Communications in Computer and Information Science 2646

Rationale

The CCIS series is devoted to the publication of proceedings of computer science conferences. Its aim is to efficiently disseminate original research results in informatics in printed and electronic form. While the focus is on publication of peer-reviewed full papers presenting mature work, inclusion of reviewed short papers reporting on work in progress is welcome, too. Besides globally relevant meetings with internationally representative program committees guaranteeing a strict peer-reviewing and paper selection process, conferences run by societies or of high regional or national relevance are also considered for publication.

Topics

The topical scope of CCIS spans the entire spectrum of informatics ranging from foundational topics in the theory of computing to information and communications science and technology and a broad variety of interdisciplinary application fields.

Information for Volume Editors and Authors

Publication in CCIS is free of charge. No royalties are paid, however, we offer registered conference participants temporary free access to the online version of the conference proceedings on SpringerLink (http://link.springer.com) by means of an http referrer from the conference website and/or a number of complimentary printed copies, as specified in the official acceptance email of the event.

CCIS proceedings can be published in time for distribution at conferences or as post-proceedings, and delivered in the form of printed books and/or electronically as USBs and/or e-content licenses for accessing proceedings at SpringerLink. Furthermore, CCIS proceedings are included in the CCIS electronic book series hosted in the SpringerLink digital library at http://link.springer.com/bookseries/7899. Conferences publishing in CCIS are allowed to use Online Conference Service (OCS) for managing the whole proceedings lifecycle (from submission and reviewing to preparing for publication) free of charge.

Publication process

The language of publication is exclusively English. Authors publishing in CCIS have to sign the Springer CCIS copyright transfer form, however, they are free to use their material published in CCIS for substantially changed, more elaborate subsequent publications elsewhere. For the preparation of the camera-ready papers/files, authors have to strictly adhere to the Springer CCIS Authors' Instructions and are strongly encouraged to use the CCIS LaTeX style files or templates.

Abstracting/Indexing

CCIS is abstracted/indexed in DBLP, Google Scholar, EI-Compendex, Mathematical Reviews, SCImago, Scopus. CCIS volumes are also submitted for the inclusion in ISI Proceedings.

How to start

To start the evaluation of your proposal for inclusion in the CCIS series, please send an e-mail to ccis@springer.com.

Juan Ignacio Godino Llorente
Editor

Automatic Assessment of Parkinsonian Speech

Second International Workshop, AAPS 2024
Cambridge, MA, USA, November 21–22, 2024
Revised Selected Papers

Springer

Editor
Juan Ignacio Godino Llorente
Universidad Politécnica de Madrid
Madrid, Spain

ISSN 1865-0929 ISSN 1865-0937 (electronic)
Communications in Computer and Information Science
ISBN 978-3-032-07082-1 ISBN 978-3-032-07083-8 (eBook)
https://doi.org/10.1007/978-3-032-07083-8

This Springer imprint is published by the registered company Springer Nature Switzerland AG
The registered company address is: Gewerbestrasse 11, 6330 Cham, Switzerland

Preface

Parkinson's disease impacts brain cells responsible for producing dopamine. Its symptoms include muscle stiffness, tremors, and changes in speech. While treatments can alleviate these symptoms following diagnosis, there is currently no cure. This makes early diagnosis crucial. Among potential biomarkers for early detection, speech remains a promising but under-researched candidate.

Despite significant progress in this area, there is still much to learn—not only about how Parkinson's disease affects speech, but also how speech characteristics correlate with disease progression. Advances in this understanding could improve the performance and reliability of automated systems designed for Parkinson's assessment and monitoring.

The 2nd Automatic Assessment of Parkinsonian Speech (AAPS 2024) workshop aimed to bring together experts from various disciplines to discuss recent developments and foster collaboration in the field of automated Parkinsonian speech assessment. This was the second of a series that was interrupted by the pandemic in 2020–2021. The long-term goal of this workshop is to develop deeper interdisciplinary knowledge of the relationship between speech and Parkinson's, which could support diagnosis, assessment, and rehabilitation, particularly in the disease's early stages.

Held over two intensive days in Cambridge, MA, USA, at the Research Laboratory of Electronics (RLE) at the Massachusetts Institute of Technology (MIT), AAPS 2024 gathered international specialists in machine learning, speech technology, phonetics, neurology, and speech therapy. The rich discussions and exchange of ideas culminated in this book, which features the most notable contributions from the workshop. Selected through a rigorous single blind peer-review process in which submissions received on average three reviews each, these papers are extended versions of the original submissions and represent key themes discussed during the event. The workshop received 13 oral presentations, from which 7 full papers were ultimately accepted for inclusion in these post-conference proceedings. An additional invited contribution was also included, which was also reviewed following the same procedure.

We extend our sincere gratitude to the Program and Organizing Committees, the reviewers for their dedication and expertise, and Springer for their professional support in producing these proceedings. We also thank all the participants and authors who contributed to the success of AAPS 2024 through their submissions and active engagement.

This workshop also honored the centennial of Kenneth Stevens, a pioneer in acoustic phonetics. Professor Stevens was the Clarence J. LeBel Professor of Electrical Engineering and Computer Science and a professor of health sciences and technology at MIT's RLE. He led the Speech Communication Group and was recognized globally for his groundbreaking work. His accolades include the National Medal of Science (1999) and the IEEE James L. Flanagan Speech and Audio Processing Award (2004).

April 2025 Juan I. Godino-Llorente

Organization

General Chairs

Stefanie Shattuck-Hufnagel	Massachusetts Institute of Technology, USA
Juan I. Godino-Llorente	Universidad Politécnica de Madrid, Spain

Scientific Secretaries

Jeung-Yoon Choi	Massachusetts Institute of Technology, USA
Julián D. Arias-Londoño	Universidad Politécnica de Madrid, Spain

Steering Committee

Jeung-Yoon Choi	Massachusetts Institute of Technology, USA
Julián D. Arias-Londoño	Universidad Politécnica de Madrid, Spain
Juan I. Godino-Llorente	Universidad Politécnica de Madrid, Spain
Mark Hasegawa-Johnson	University of Illinois Urbana-Champaign, USA
Stefanie Shattuck-Hufnagel	Massachusetts Institute of Technology, USA

Program Committee

Alberto Abad	University of Lisbon, Portugal
Ascensión Gallardo-Antolín	Universidad Carlos III de Madrid, Spain
Daryush Metha	Harvard University, USA
Germán Castellanos-Domínguez	Universidad Nacional de Colombia, Colombia
Jeung-Yoon Choi	Massachusetts Institute of Technology, USA
Jiri Mekyska	Brno University of Technology, Czech Republic
Jorge A. Gómez-García	Spanish National Research Council, Spain
Jose L. Blanco Murillo	Universidad Politécnica de Madrid, Spain
Juan I. Godino-Llorente	Universidad Politécnica de Madrid, Spain
Julián D. Arias-Londoño	Universidad Politécnica de Madrid, Spain
Laureano Moro-Velazquez	Johns Hopkins University, USA
Mark Hasegawa-Johnson	University of Illinois Urbana-Champaign, USA
Matías Zañartu	Universidad Técnica Federico Santa María, Chile
Nicholas Cummins	King's College London, UK

Sponsors

MISTI Global Seed Funds Award
Massachusetts Institute of Technology
Universidad Politécnica de Madrid
European Lab for Learning and Intelligent Systems

This activity is framed in the MISTI project "*Objective evaluation of neurological disorders from the speech*" funded by MISTI Global Seed Funds Award, which was developed jointly by Massachusetts Institute of Technology and Universidad Politécnica de Madrid.

Contents

Speech-Based Detection of Parkinson's Disease in Low- Resourced Languages: A 20-Year Journey Through Speech Processing and Machine Learning Techniques

Luis Pinto-Coelho(✉)

ISEP, Polytechnic of Porto, Porto, Portugal
lfc@isep.ipp.pt

Abstract. Parkinson's disease frequently manifests with vocal symptoms, such as monotonicity, breathiness, and irregular pitch, all correlating with motor impairments and detectable through speech features. Advances in signal processing and machine learning have made these vocal markers a promising tool for noninvasive, cost-effective screening. However, several challenges limit the clinical adoption of these tools. Limited data and the higher focus on English-speaking populations, raise concerns about model's performance across languages. In low resourced languages, this can hinder the clinical validation of such opportunities. This paper examines the development of resources and tools for PD voice-based characterization in European Portuguese over the last two decades. Beyond diagnostics, it explores the potential of vocal biomarkers as real-time feedback mechanisms for PD management. Finally, it addresses the ongoing challenges and limitations to achieving universal adoption of voice-based PD diagnostic systems.

Keywords: Parkinson's · Speech · Classification · Phonetic · Portuguese

1 Introduction

The global prevalence of neurological diseases continues to rise, with Parkinson's disease (PD) consistently representing a significant portion of these cases. Although clinical diagnosis of PD can be highly accurate, it is often made at a stage when the patient's functionality is already compromised. Early detection and widespread screening are critical for improving prognoses and treatment outcomes. Over the past few decades, voice-based diagnostics for PD have gained significant attention, largely due to the distinct vocal symptoms—such as monotonicity, breathiness, and pitch irregularity—that often accompany the disease. These correlate with the motor impairments PD causes, prompting researchers to explore acoustic markers using signal processing and, more recently, machine learning techniques [1].

Despite its feasibility and advantages—particularly its low cost and non-invasive nature—voice-based PD characterization faces challenges that have limited its clinical validation and adoption. One central limitation is that existing datasets are not extensive

J. I. Godino Llorente (Ed.): AAPS 2024, CCIS 2646, pp. 1–12, 2026.
https://doi.org/10.1007/978-3-032-07083-8_1

and many of them were collected under very distinct conditions and according with different scripts. In addition, much of the existing research mainly focus on English, raising concerns about the effectiveness of PD decision models across languages. On the other hand, models developed primarily with low-resourced language data may underperform when tested in larger corpora, in a diverse linguistic context. This results in sparce developments, hindering the clinical usage of such systems on a global scale.

This paper focus on resources, features and tools for voice-based PD characterization in European Portuguese (EP). It will also address existing related challenges.

2 European Portuguese Resources and Tools for PD

EP phonology diverges significantly from other Romance languages through several distinctive features. The language is characterized by extensive vowel reduction, where unstressed vowels frequently centralize or disappear completely, creating a uniquely compressed sound profile. This vowel reduction leads to a high frequency of schwa sounds and near-silent vowels that are markedly different from Spanish, Italian, or French phonetic systems. From an acoustic perspective, there are also variations in vowel formants when comparing Portuguese and Spanish [2], which can have implications of speech dynamics.

Nasal phonemes play a particularly crucial role in Portuguese phonology. The language possesses a robust system of nasal vowels and diphthongs that are more complex and prevalent than in other Romance languages. These nasal sounds create a distinctive acoustic texture that immediately distinguishes Portuguese from its linguistic relatives, with nasalization occurring more extensively and systematically.

The consonantal system of EP also exhibits unique characteristics, particularly in its treatment of certain consonant clusters and pronunciation patterns. EP demonstrates a tendency toward consonant deletion and elision that is more aggressive than in other Romance languages, further contributing to its phonological distinctiveness. The result is a linguistic sound system that, while sharing Romance language roots, presents a markedly different auditory experience from Spanish or Italian pronunciation.

When comparing EP and Brazilian Portuguese (BP) differ significantly in phonology. EP features strong vowel reduction, often turning unstressed vowels into schwa-like sounds or eliding them, while BP maintains clearer vowel articulation. BP has stronger nasalization, with nasal vowels being more monophthongal, whereas EP tends to produce nasalized diphthongs. Prosodically, EP is more syllable-timed with greater intonational variation, while BP is stress-timed with a more rhythmic, singsong-like quality. In sibilants, EP favors a palatalized [ʃ] in coda position, while BP varies between [s] and [ʃ] depending on the region. Rhotics also differ: EP often uses a uvular fricative [ʁ] and weakens coda _r_, whereas BP shows more regional variation, including alveolar flaps [ɾ] and uvular realizations [ʁ]. BP also simplifies consonant clusters by inserting epenthetic vowels and exhibits stronger palatalization of _t_ and _d_ before front vowels, turning them into [tʃ] and [dʒ] (e.g., _tia_ [ˈtʃia], _dia_ [ˈdʒia]). These differences contribute to EP's more closed and conservative articulation and BP's more open and fluid sound [3].

2.1 Resources

The majority of PD speech and language resources are available for English language and, while EP and English share some phonological features due to their Indo-European roots, the differences in vowel systems, consonant sounds, prosody, and intonation make them quite distinct from a phonological perspective. Modern language and speech processing systems rely heavily on large volumes of high-quality, annotated data. For these purposes, EP remains a low-resource language with a notable scarcity of well-annotated voice datasets. This limitation is even more pronounced in a disease context, where sample size small. In the case of PD, the earliest recorded dataset in EP was reported by Proença et al. (2014) [4]. The database is composed of 22 speakers with PD (12 females and 10 males), from ages 50 to 80, with disease development at stages 2 and 3 of the Hohen and Yahr (H-Y) scale. The recording script included phonetically rich sentences and isolated words. The recordings were collected using at 48 kHz.

Another collection, the FraLusoPark dataset, is described by Pinto et al. (2017) [5] covering a cohort of 60 individuals (with age ranging from 52 to 76). For each patient, recordings were performed in the ON state (following at least 1 h after the administration of the usual medication) and in the OFF state (at least 12 h after withdrawal of all therapy drugs). Participants followed increasingly complex phonation tasks. They began with repetitions of the sustained vowel /a/, followed by two repetitions of the maximum phonation time. Next, they performed oral diadochokinesia by repeating the word "pataka" at a fast rate for 30 s. Reading 10 words and 10 sentences followed. Participants then read the text "The North Wind and the Sun," and engaged in storytelling. Finally, a set of prosodically varied sentences were read. Acoustic data was acquired in a quiet room using a sampling rate of 48 kHz.

In 2019, another EP speech dataset is reported in Braga et al. [6]. It is composed of 30 healthy speakers (21 females and 9 males), from ages 20 to 71 (mean 41.68, standard deviation 14.1), containing 785 speech lines, totaling 28.2 min of play time. The data collection was developed to extend the one in [4] and for this purpose, a similar script, selecting the most common and phonetically rich speech sentences was created. These samples were recorded at a 44.1 kHz sample rate. This dataset has been used to create a control group to be used in conjunction with Proença et al. (2014) [4].

As described, these datasets were acquired in distinct conditions, with diverse scripts and have been labeled according with distinct scales. None is publicly available. Concerning Brazilian Portuguese (BP) and Angolan Portuguese (AP), no speech datasets have been currently reported within the scope of speech-based PD detection.

2.2 Features

The impact of PD in speech was identified decades ago, with the majority of individuals developing hypokinetic dysarthria at some point. Reduced speech loudness, monotone and monoloud prosody, abnormal rates of speech, including fast rushes of speech, and imprecise articulation have been reported as prominent indicators with phonatory impairments being the most frequently occurring and perceptually salient [7, 8].

A key indicator of hypokinetic dysarthria, characterized by reduced range and velocity of articulatory movements. Due to articulatory undershoot, speakers fail to reach the canonical formant frequencies, leading to vowel frequency centralization. When exploring formant vowel space, in the EP data set described in [4], it is possible to observe this clear effect, with a successively reduce vowel frequency space correlated with disease progression ratings (for both men and women).

Speech dynamics features can provide additional insights. In the context of PD detection, formant transitions and speaking rate are popular metrics but they can vary significantly across languages. Formant transitions, which reflect changes in the resonant frequencies of the vocal tract as speakers move between vowel sounds, play a critical role in the clarity and intelligibility of speech. Especially in its Brazilian variant, the language has a relatively large inventory of vowel sounds, including nasalized vowels, that require precise articulatory control to maintain distinctiveness. In individuals with PD, reduced articulatory precision can lead to flatter or slower formant transitions, making vowel sounds less distinct and more centralized. This is particularly important in Portuguese, where vowel distinctions often carry semantic weight. For Portuguese speakers with PD, these articulation changes may lead to misunderstandings or reduced intelligibility, as they are unable to maintain the expected distinct vowel qualities.

Speaking rate is another critical metric in PD. EP, like many Romance languages, is considered syllable-timed, unlike stress-timed languages like English [9]. Parkinson's-related disruptions to speaking rate—such as slowing down, irregular bursts of speech, or prolonged pauses—can interrupt this rhythmic flow, making the speech sound uneven or dysrhythmic, with impact on the natural voice pleasantness [10]. In addition, irregularities in rate and rhythm are often more perceptible in a syllable-timed language, providing another diagnostic cue.

With higher language independence, speech perturbation measures, such as shimmer and jitter, can provide important insights into the important aspects of speech production. Despite their popularity, along with MFCC and harmonic to noise ratio, other speech features can bring additional insights to detect PD. For example, a comparative analysis of the articulation transition characteristics has been reported [11], showing that the number of articulation transitions and the trend of the fundamental frequency curve, capturing energy content in transitions from unvoiced to voiced segments and vice versa, are significantly different between HC speakers and PD patients. In addition, abnormalities in the smoothness of formant transitions (e.g., steeper or more irregular slopes) can indicate impaired speech motor control. Also, glottal features, estimated using methods like iterative adaptive inverse filtering (IAIF) and quasi-closed phase (QCP) glottal inverse filtering, have been found effective in detecting PD. These features are used in both traditional and deep learning models to improve classification accuracy [12]. Table 1 presents a list of speech features that have been proven to be related to PD detection, often reported with good classification performance. These, and many others, not listed, show the dimension of variable space that speech offers, but also demonstrate the feasibility of using speech as a PD biomarker. Concerning EP, an extensive comparison of features has been performed with the eGeMAPS set, extracted with OpenSmile [13], leading to a classification performance of 95.27% accuracy on the identification of PD medication effects and states [14].

Table 1. Popular speech features for the detection of PD patterns.

Category	Static Features	Dynamic Features
Pitch-Related (F0)	Mean, median, and standard deviation of F0; Maximum and minimum F0	Jitter (variability in F0); F0 contour smoothness (slope, curvature)
Amplitude-Related	Mean, median, and standard deviation of amplitude; Maximum and minimum amplitude	Shimmer (variability in amplitude); Amplitude modulation patterns
Formant-Related	Mean values of formant frequencies (F1, F2, F3); Formant bandwidths	Formant transition trajectories (slope, curvature, duration); Coarticulation patterns
Temporal Features	Speech rate (words/syllables per second); Pause frequency and duration	Variability in phoneme duration; Rhythmic patterns and irregularities
Voice Quality Features	Harmonic-to-Noise Ratio (HNR); Glottal flow parameters	HNR during transitions; Perturbation measures (jitter, shimmer) during speech
Spectral Features	Mel-Frequency Cepstral Coefficients (MFCCs); Spectral centroid, spread, skewness	Spectral rate of change, Dynamic time warping (DTW) of spectral patterns
Articulatory/Phonetic Transition Features	Voice Onset Time (VOT); Articulatory precision (eg., clarity of consonants)	Formant transition smoothness; Coarticulation patterns and timing; Transition duration and variability
Prosodic Features	Mean and variability of intonation contours; Stress patterns (intensity, timing)	Intonation contour smoothness; Variability in stress timing and intensity
Nonlinear/Complexity Features	Recurrence Quantification Analysis (RQA); Detrended Fluctuation Analysis (DFA)	Complexity of speech dynamics (e.g., entropy); Stability of speech patterns
Dysphonia Features	Perturbation measures (jitter, shimmer); Noise-to-harmonic ratio	Perturbation measures during transitions; Variability in dysphonia measures,

While high-dimensional feature sets extracted by tools like openSMILE can capture subtle acoustic characteristics, they often necessitate dimensionality reduction techniques like PCA or LASSO regression to manage computational complexity and prevent overfitting. However, this reduction process transforms the original features into abstract components or selects subset features through complex mathematical operations, making it challenging to interpret how specific acoustic properties contribute to the final analysis. This trade-off between computational efficiency and interpretability can complicate the practical application of findings, particularly in fields where understanding the underlying acoustic mechanisms is crucial.

Modern end-to-end deep learning approaches and embedding-based models can also effectively capture complex acoustic patterns and achieve strong performance in speech tasks. However, their black-box nature and learned representations are inherently opaque, making it difficult to understand which specific acoustic features drive predictions or how the model arrives at its decisions, limiting their applicability in clinical contexts where interpretability is essential.

2.3 Tools and Models

To expand the existing datasets, it is important to create platforms that allow users to easily contribute. In this context, a mobile app was developed, as described in [15], featuring a speech recording feature, allowing users to provide their voice in a simple and practical way. This enables doctors to monitor the evolution of acoustic features asynchronously, providing valuable insight into disease progression over time. Additionally, it features a wide range of functionalities, as can be observed in Fig. 1, enhancing neurodegenerative disease management. Beyond speech recording, users can also log symptom details, which is especially beneficial for refining treatment plans. Additionally, the app offers cognitive training games, with scores that may serve as indicators of disease progression. Built on a Python-based framework, the app incorporates signal processing techniques and machine learning algorithms to analyze user data effectively. The described app can work as a centralized platform, that simplifies data collection and facilitates information exchange between patients and healthcare providers, enhancing neurodegenerative disease management. Furthermore, it can serve as a test bed for current research on PD detection and management technologies beyond laboratory settings, where, for example, a trial group of users can access specific functionalities.

In [16], focusing only on speech data, using the EP PD speech dataset described in [4], twelve speech perturbation features were extracted, including shimmer, jitter, and the harmonics-to-noise ratio, along with their associated variations. For comparison, a healthy control (HC) group consisting of 22 individuals (11M, 11F) aged between 20 and 73 years was established. For each participant, one minute of spontaneous speech was recorded without any script or restrictions. A similar set of features was extracted from the HC group recordings. To differentiate PD patients from the healthy control group, an ANOVA test was conducted on the values of each feature. The analysis revealed that shimmer local and shimmer APQ11 exhibited statistically distinct distributions ($p < 0.0001$), allowing for effective discrimination between the two groups.

Using the same dataset, a more comprehensive approach is described in [6] (an improved and extended version of [17]). In this case, three datasets are integrated for PD classification: one in English and two in EP. These studies represent the first multilingual approach where distinct languages were used interchangeably as acoustic sources for biomarker extraction. From these corpora, a set of 19 features was extracted, focusing primarily on perturbation measures, with gender also included as a variable (0-male, 1-female). Before applying machine learning algorithms, exploratory data analysis was conducted to better understand the data. Principal Component Analysis (PCA) and linear

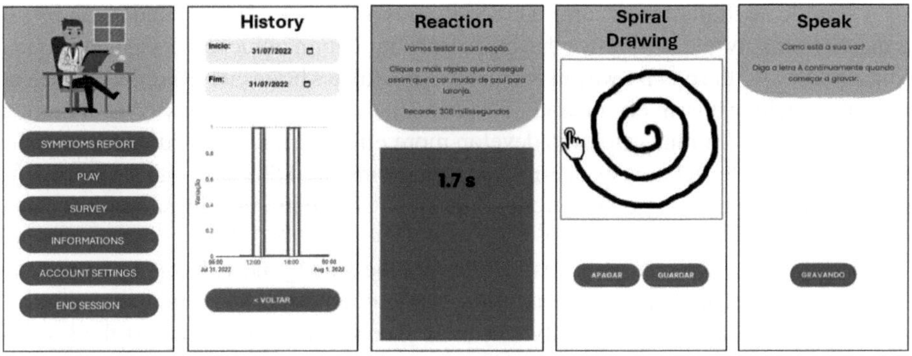

Fig. 1. Screenshots of the mobile application "Mentalist", developed for the management of neurodegenerative diseases. From left to right: Main menu; History for a given symptom; Reaction time game; Spiral drawing activity; Speech data collection function.

regression analyses were employed to investigate whether any linearly separable classes or patterns were present; however, none were found. Five classification algorithms were tested: Naïve Bayes, Perceptron, a small Artificial Neural Network (ANN), Support Vector Machine (SVM), and Random Forest (RF). As anticipated, the nonlinear algorithms outperformed the linear models, warranting additional refinement. Final model performance was assessed using the Leave-One-Out cross-validation method, with the RF approach achieving the highest accuracy at 99.94%.

Beyond ANN, more complex models such as deep neural networks (DNN), due to their ability to deal with complex patterns, have also been applied to analyze PD speech data [18]. From the dataset in [4], features followed the methodology outlined in [6] and then processed through a PCA stage to optimize variance. Due to the limited number of records, a custom CNN architecture was carefully designed and fine-tuned to balance high discrimination power with low parameter requirements. This model achieved an accuracy of 93.4% for a binary classification. For multiclass classification, aimed at assessing disease progression scores, the model attained an accuracy of 84.7%. Extending the range of applications, in [19], the possibility of using speech as a PD biomarker in a feedback loop to fine-tune deep brain stimulation (DBS) is considered. The current DBS systems have several limitations that still need to be addressed. One of the main challenges is that most systems operate in an open-loop mode, where stimulation parameters are pre-set by a clinician and remain unchanged between consultations. This approach is highly limited in an initial stage, immediately after surgery, and fails to account for the dynamic nature of PD symptoms, which fluctuate throughout the day and progress over time. Additionally, the inability to adapt stimulation in real time makes it difficult to manage adverse effects, including those affecting speech, which are often caused by continuous, fixed-amplitude stimulation. Many studies report that DBS, especially when targeting the subthalamic nucleus (STN), can have negative effects on speech, such as worsening speech intelligibility and articulation [20, 21]. High-frequency stimulation and certain anatomical targets like the globus pallidus internus (GPi) have been associated with deteriorations in speech quality.

A significant limitation of current DBS systems is the lack of a clear understanding of its mechanisms. While it is known that electrical stimulation influences local neurons and axonal pathways, the precise way in which DBS modulates brain circuits remains unclear. Multiple mechanisms likely operate simultaneously, adding complexity to treatment optimization and limiting efforts to develop more effective and targeted therapies. This is particularly relevant for speech-related symptoms, as DBS can either improve or impair speech, depending on electrode placement, stimulation settings, and individual patient factors.

The impact of DBS on speech is highly variable among individuals. Some patients experience significant speech deterioration, while others may see minimal changes or even improvements. This variability can be influenced by factors such as the specific DBS settings, the anatomical target, and individual patient characteristics [22]. Patients often report more severe speech disturbances post-DBS, with common issues including low volume and slurred speech, which can significantly impact social interactions and quality of life [23].

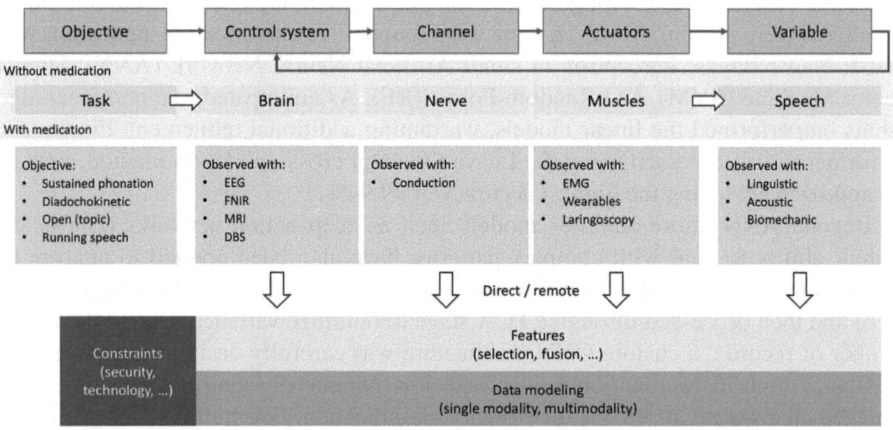

Fig. 2. Speech production process observed from a control systems' perspective, highlighting information sources that can serve as disease biomarkers.

Currently, parameter selection after surgery is based on a trial-and-error approach, relying on qualitative clinical evaluations. Once parameters are set, they remain fixed until the next consultation, despite ongoing fluctuations in symptoms. The lack of personalized therapy in DBS highlights the need for adaptive solutions that can dynamically adjust to individual patient needs over time. In addition to these functional challenges, hardware limitations present another hurdle. Implantable Pulse Generators (IPGs), which deliver electrical stimulation, face constraints related to battery life, memory capacity, and computational power.

Despite the known deleterious effect of DBS in speech production, the use of speech as a biomarker for DBS parameter tuning is a promising opportunity. Speech production is highly sensitive to neuromodulation, making it a valuable, non-invasive marker for monitoring treatment effects and adjusting stimulation parameters. By analyzing speech features such as articulation, phonation, and prosody, the development of real-time, speech-driven adaptive DBS systems is envisioned. This dual relationship— where speech can both reflect PD symptoms and be directly altered by DBS—makes it essential to develop careful calibration methods that account for these bidirectional effects. In fact, low-frequency and bilateral DBS have been associated with relative improvements in phonation and articulation [22].

An obstacle in advancing speech-based DBS technology is the limited availability of high-quality, long-term data. Machine learning (ML) is increasingly being explored to enhance DBS therapies, but training robust ML models requires large datasets, particularly those with extensive longitudinal speech recordings. This would allow DBS parameters, such as current, voltage, frequency, electrode, or duty cycle to be correlated with speech features.

In more general terms, speech generation is a complex task. Beyond its commonly considered acoustic realization, the production process offers much more information, as illustrated in Fig. 2, which depicts various physiological signals that can be potential sources of pathological patterns.

The adoption of closed-loop speech-based DBS systems can mark a critical step toward overcoming the challenges of traditional DBS, allowing dynamic adjustment that minimize adverse effects and enhance disease management, leading to more personalized, effective, and adaptable neuromodulation therapies.

2.4 Limitations

Speech-based classification of PD has shown promise in research settings as a noninvasive, low-cost, and accessible method for early detection and monitoring. Yet, its clinical implementation has been limited due to several challenges:

1) Variability in Speech Patterns: PD affects individuals differently, leading to significant variations in speech symptoms such as dysarthria, reduced articulation, and vocal tremors. These variations can be influenced by factors like disease stage, medication effects, and individual speaking habits, making it difficult to develop universally applicable models.
2) Limited Standardization and Validation: Current studies often use different speech tasks, recording environments, and feature extraction techniques, leading to inconsistent results. The lack of standardized protocols for data collection and analysis hinders the reproducibility of findings and the establishment of clinically validated models.
3) High Accuracy Requirements for Clinical Use: While many machine learning models achieve promising results in research, clinical deployment requires near-perfect reliability to avoid misdiagnoses. Ensuring sensitivity and specificity comparable to existing diagnostic tools remains a significant hurdle, especially when distinguishing PD from other neurological conditions with overlapping speech impairments.
4) Ethical and Data Privacy Concerns: Speech data is highly sensitive and can reveal personal health information beyond PD detection. Ensuring compliance with data protection regulations such as GDPR and HIPAA is essential. Additionally, ethical concerns regarding consent, bias in datasets, and potential misuse of voice-based biomarkers need to be carefully addressed.

5) Limited Clinical Evidence of Long-Term Benefit: While preliminary studies suggest speech-based biomarkers can detect PD, there is limited longitudinal evidence demonstrating their effectiveness in tracking disease progression or improving patient outcomes. Clinical trials are needed to establish their role in long-term disease management.
6) Integration into Clinical Workflow and International Guidelines: For speech-based detection to be widely adopted, it must seamlessly integrate with existing diagnostic and monitoring tools. This requires compatibility with electronic health record systems, training for clinicians, and alignment with international guidelines such as those from the Movement Disorder Society (MDS) or the World Health Organization (WHO).
7) Software as a Medical Device (SaMD) Requirements: Regulatory approval is necessary for speech-based tools to be used in clinical practice. Meeting the requirements of agencies like the FDA and EMA involves rigorous validation, risk assessment, and compliance with medical device standards. The evolving regulatory landscape for AI-diagnostics further complicates approval pathways.
8) Validation of Language-Independent Approaches: Many speech-based PD detection models are trained on specific languages, which may limit their generalizability across diverse linguistic populations. Speech characteristics such as phonetics, intonation, and prosody vary significantly between languages, potentially affecting model performance. Developing language-independent approaches or methods adaptable to multiple languages is crucial to ensuring equitable and global applicability. Large-scale multilingual datasets and cross-linguistic validation studies are necessary to address this challenge.
9) Challenges in Differential Diagnosis: Many neurological and neurodegenerative disorders, such as atypical Parkinsonian syndromes, amyotrophic lateral sclerosis (ALS) [24], multiple system atrophy (MSA), and essential tremor, can affect speech in ways that overlap with PD-related symptoms. Additionally, non-neurological conditions like vocal cord disorders or age-related speech changes can further complicate differentiation. Ensuring that models can accurately distinguish PD from these conditions is critical. This requires diverse datasets, advanced feature selection, and multimodal approaches that integrate other biomarkers, such as imaging or genetic data, to enhance diagnostic specificity.

These are some of the challenges take must be tackled so speech-based classification of PD can transition from research settings to real-world clinical applications.

3 Final Remarks

The ability to detect PD through speech patterns opens exciting new possibilities for early diagnosis, intervention and monitoring. To maximize the impact of these tools, it is crucial to develop simple, interpretable, and data-driven models that are both accessible and effective. However, realizing their full potential requires a unified scientific effort. Standardized data collection campaigns—incorporating shared protocols such as evaluation scales, task guidelines, and medication tracking—are essential for ensuring consistency and reliability. Additionally, embracing linguistic diversity is critical to making these technologies globally applicable. Ethical integrity and regulatory compliance must remain at the forefront to maintain trust and reliability in these solutions. The future of Parkinson's detection depends on a collective commitment to advancing these technologies, bridging the gap between laboratory research and real-world clinical impact. By fostering collaboration, it is possible to transform innovative speech-based tools into life-changing solutions for patients worldwide.

References

1. Pinto-Coelho, L., Garcia-Mateo, C.: Speech based evaluation of neurological diseases. In: Computer-Speech and Language (2022)
2. Chládková, K., Escudero, P.: Comparing vowel perception and production in Spanish and Portuguese: European versus Latin American dialects. J. Acoust. Soc. Am. **131**, EL119–EL125 (2012). https://doi.org/10.1121/1.3674991
3. Escudero, P., Boersma, P., Rauber, A.S., Bion, R.A.H.: A cross-dialect acoustic description of vowels: Brazilian and European Portuguese. J. Acoust. Soc. Am. **126**, 1379–1393 (2009). https://doi.org/10.1121/1.3180321
4. Proença, J., Veiga, A., Candeias, S., Lemos, J., Januário, C., Perdigão, F.: Characterizing Parkinson's disease speech by acoustic and phonetic features. In: Computational Processing of the Portuguese Language: 11th International Conference, PROPOR 2014, São Carlos/SP, Brazil, 6–8 October 2014. Proceedings, vol. 11, pp. 24–35. Springer, Heidelberg (2014)
5. Pinto, S., et al.: Dysarthria in individuals with Parkinson's disease: a protocol for a binational, cross-sectional, case-controlled study in French and European Portuguese (FraLusoPark). BMJ Open **6**, e012885 (2016). https://doi.org/10.1136/bmjopen-2016-012885
6. Braga, D., Madureira, A.M., Coelho, L., Ajith, R.: Automatic detection of Parkinson's disease based on acoustic analysis of speech. Eng. Appl. Artif. Intell. **77**, 148–158 (2019). https://doi.org/10.1016/j.engappai.2018.09.018
7. Logemann, J.A., Fisher, H.B., Boshes, B., Blonsky, E.R.: Frequency and cooccurrence of vocal tract dysfunctions in the speech of a large sample of Parkinson patients. J. Speech Hear. Disord. **43**, 45–47 (1978). https://doi.org/10.1044/jshd.4301.47
8. Ludlow, C.L., Connor, N.P., Bassich, C.J.: Speech timing in Parkinson's and Huntington's disease. Brain Lang. **32**, 195–214 (1987)
9. Wetzels, L., Costa, J., Menuzzi, S.: The Handbook of Portuguese Linguistics. John Wiley & Sons, Inc., Hoboken (2016)
10. Coelho, L., Braga, D., Dias, M., Garcia-Mateo, C.: An automatic voice pleasantness classification system based on prosodic and acoustic patterns of voice preference. In: Proceedings of Interspeech, Florence (2011)
11. Quan, C., Ren, K., Luo, Z.: A deep learning based method for parkinson's disease detection using dynamic features of speech. IEEE Access. **9**, 10239–10252 (2021). https://doi.org/10.1109/ACCESS.2021.3051432
12. Narendra, N.P., Schuller, B., Alku, P.: The detection of parkinson's disease from speech using voice source information. IEEE/ACM Trans. Audio Speech Lang. Process. **29**, 1925–1936 (2021). https://doi.org/10.1109/TASLP.2021.3078364
13. Eyben, F., Weninger, F., Gross, F., Schuller, B.: Recent developments in openSMILE, the munich open-source multimedia feature extractor. In: Proceedings of the 21st ACM International Conference on Multimedia, pp. 835–838. Association for Computing Machinery, New York (2013). https://doi.org/10.1145/2502081.2502224
14. Pompili, A., et al.: Assessment of Parkinson's disease medication state through automatic speech analysis. In: Presented at the Interspeech, 25 October 2020 (2020). https://doi.org/10.21437/Interspeech.2020-2726

15. Santos, P., Pinto-Coelho, L.: A gamified application for multimodal diagnosis and monitoring of neurodegenerative diseases. In: Presented at the Simpósio de Engenharia Informática, Porto, Portugal (2023)
16. Teixeira, J., ET AL.: Towards an objective criteria for the diagnosis of Parkinson disease based on speech assessment. In: XXXV Congreso anual de la Sociedad Española de Ingeniería Biomédica: Libro de actas, pp. 319–322. Argitalpen Zerbitzua (2017)
17. Braga, D., Madureira, A.M., Coelho, L., Abraham, A.: Neurodegenerative diseases detection through voice analysis. In: Abraham, A., Muhuri, P.Kr., Muda, A.K., Gandhi, N. (eds.) Hybrid Intelligent Systems, pp. 213–223. Springer, Cham (2018)
18. Sousa, L., Braga, D., Madureira, A., Coelho, L., Renna, F.: Characterizing Parkinson's disease from speech samples using deep structured learning. In: Madureira, A.M., Abraham, A., Gandhi, N., Silva, C., Antunes, M. (eds.) Proceedings of the Tenth International Conference on Soft Computing and Pattern Recognition (SoCPaR 2018), pp. 137–146. Springer, Cham (2020). https://doi.org/10.1007/978-3-030-17065-3_14
19. Oliveira, A.M., Coelho, L., Carvalho, E., Ferreira-Pinto, M.J., Vaz, R., Aguiar, P.: Machine learning for adaptive deep brain stimulation in Parkinson's disease: closing the loop. J. Neurol. **270**, 5313–5326 (2023). https://doi.org/10.1007/s00415-023-11873-1
20. Baudouin, R., Lechien, J.R., Carpentier, L., Gurruchaga, J., Lisan, Q., Hans, S.: Deep brain stimulation impact on voice and speech quality in parkinson's disease: a systematic review. Otolaryngol.--Head Neck Surg. **168**, 307–318 (2023). https://doi.org/10.1177/01945998221120189
21. Wang, E.Q., Mullen, M., Karl, J.A., Verhagen Metman, L.A.: The impact on speech with different deep brain stimulation settings in Parkinson's disease. J. Acoust. Soc. Am. **152**, A137–A137 (2022). https://doi.org/10.1121/10.0015802
22. Tabari, F., Berger, J.I., Flouty, O., Copeland, B., Greenlee, J.D., Johari, K.: Speech, voice, and language outcomes following deep brain stimulation: a systematic review. PLoS ONE **19**, e0302739 (2024). https://doi.org/10.1371/journal.pone.0302739
23. Wertheimer, J., et al.: The impact of STN deep brain stimulation on speech in individuals with Parkinson's disease: the patient's perspective. Parkinsonism Relat. Disord. **20**, 1065–1070 (2014). https://doi.org/10.1016/j.parkreldis.2014.06.010
24. Vieira, H., Costa, N., Sousa, T., Reis, S., Coelho, L.: Voice-based classification of amyotrophic lateral sclerosis: where are we and where are we going? A systematic review. NDD **19**, 163–170 (2019). https://doi.org/10.1159/000506259

Speech Pattern Variability in the Speech Accessibility Project

Heejin Kim[1](✉), Clarion Mendes[1], Mark Hasegawa-Johnson[1], and Lorraine Ramig[2]

[1] University of Illinois, Urbana, IL 61801, USA
{hkim17,cmendes2,jhasegaw}@illinois.edu
[2] LSVT Global, Boulder, CO, USA
ramig@colorado.edu

Abstract. This article reports on speech characteristics observed in recordings of speech by people with Parkinson's disease. Participants included people who self-reported diagnoses including Classic Idiopathic Parkinson's (IPD) disease, Progressive Supranuclear Palsy (PSP), Multi-system Atrophy (MSA), Cortical Basal Degeneration (CBD), implanted systems for Deep Brain Stimulation (DBS) [1], and people both currently taking and currently not taking levodopa [2]. For reasons of participant privacy, individual self-diagnoses are not included in distributed metadata. A large majority of the recorded samples exhibit the acoustic correlates of hypokinetic dysarthria classically observed in IPD, including reduced loudness, monotone, breathy, hoarse voicing, imprecise consonantal articulation, and increased, decreased or variable speaking rate [3]. A small minority of speech samples (15%) exhibit samples observed in Parkinsonisms (Atypical Parkinsonian Syndromes) including PSP, MSA, CBD, as well as DBS [4–6]. These disorders have been associated with a range of hypokinetic, spastic and ataxic dysarthria, stuttering, disordered articulation characterized by articulatory imprecision, vocal strain or spasticity, and disordered rate.

Keywords: Parkinson's disease · hypokinetic dysarthria · accessibility

1 Introduction

Effective automatic speech recognition (ASR) allows you to use your smart speaker or other device to change the channel, dictate text messages, transcribe a meeting or lecture, get global position information while driving, translate your speech from one language to another, or even take a group photo while you're in the group. Many people with Parkinson's disease (PD), cerebral palsy and other neuromotor disorders would like to use speech recognition, but it doesn't work for them. As reported in [7], ASR error rates for people without speech disabilities dropped from 10% to 1.4% between 2008 and 2023. During the same period of time, ASR error rates for people with cerebral palsy improved considerably, but not at the same rate or from the same baseline as error rates for people without speech disability or difference: by 2023, the best published ASR

J. I. Godino Llorente (Ed.): AAPS 2024, CCIS 2646, pp. 13–30, 2026.
https://doi.org/10.1007/978-3-032-07083-8_2

error rate for people with cerebral palsy was 17.8% [8]. ASR similarly fails for people with Parkinson's disease. In a study of two ASR architectures, Moro-Velazquez et al. [9] found that the error rate for people with Parkinson's was between 20 to 100% higher than that for age-matched, gender-matched speakers with no diagnosed motor disorder, even though all of the speech samples were judged to be intelligible by human listener.

A plausible and well-supported explanation for the relative underperformance of ASR for people with Parkinson's disease is the variability in speech patterns associated with Parkinson's disease when combined with other disorders, together with the relative paucity of relevant speech data in the training databases used for most ASR systems. The effect of Parkinson's disease on speech was recorded in the earliest descriptions of the disease [10]. Such historical reports of disordered speech include vocal tremor [11], irregular rhythm, highly variable speaking rate that may start slow and speed up [12], voice quality that may be breathy, hoarse, or aphonic [12, 13], and articulation that may alternate between a form that is greatly reduced and a form with considerable degrees of stuttering-like disfluencies and repetition [12, 14]. The characteristic intonational contour of Parkinson's disease was reported to be a reduced total pitch range and a reduction in the number of pitch accents [12], resulting in a characteristic flat contour that has been called "monopitch" [13]. These many different speech patterns typical of Parkinson's disease may be loosely grouped into atypical voice quality (dysphonia), atypical articulation (dysarthria), and atypical prosody (dysprosody). The effect of dysarthria on speech intelligibility is immediate: intelligibility may be one of the most reliable measures of dysarthria severity, as measured either subjectively or objectively by human listeners [15] or objectively using ASR [16]. The effect of dysphonia on speech intelligibility is less direct [17]. One of the most salient features of dysphonia in Parkinson's disease is reduced vocal loudness, which reduces the transcription ability of either ASR [18] or human listeners [19] under typical listening conditions, but this effect is masked in many published studies that use atypical listening conditions, e.g., playback volume adjusted for maximum intelligibility by a listener using headphones. Dysprosody unaccompanied by dysphonia or dysarthria may cause no intelligibility impairment for human listeners [20]; its effect on ASR has not been measured, but may depend on the type of machine learning algorithms used by the ASR [9].

Like all artificial intelligence systems, ASR is adjusted to work well for speech samples in a training database. When tested on speech outside its training database, it works well only if the test samples are acoustically similar to speech in the training data. The remarkable improvements observed in ASR for people without disabilities between 2008 and 2023 can be explained by the equally remarkable improvements in training data for people without speech disabilities. In 2008, the largest standard database of typical speech was the Switchboard corpus [21], containing 300 h of speech from 500 people; in 2015, most ASR research programs switched to the then-new Librispeech corpus, containing 960 h of speech from 1200 people [22]. During the same 15-year period, the largest widely available corpus containing both training and testing speech from people with dysarthria was the UA-Speech corpus [23], containing 22 h of speech from 16 people: almost two orders of magnitude less data than the standard corpora used to train non-dysarthric ASR. The small size of available training data is an adequate explanation for the less-impressive performance improvements observed for dysarthric ASR relative to typical ASR.

The Speech Accessibility Project (SAP) is an attempt to responsibly collect, curate, and distribute atypical speech (primarily dysarthric, but also including other neuromotor conditions that affect intelligibility) at a scale large enough to significantly improve the error rates of standard speech technology for people with speech-related disabilities. Participants are asked to sign up for the project even if they don't think their speech is impacted by their diagnosis, and for this reason, 1341 people with Parkinson's were screened by November, 2024, of whom 473 were approved to participate, and 366 completed the protocol. As of November, 2024, SAP had recorded the speech of 847 people, including 366 with PD. Data that has been fully annotated and is being distributed for free to researchers includes 334 h of speech from 428 people, most of whom have PD. All researchers sign a data use agreement before being given access to the corpus. In order to permit the distribution of these data to as many research teams as possible, metadata distributed with the corpus include as little participant-provided information as possible: of particular relevance to this paper, the available metadata does not specify whether a participant has been diagnosed with Idiopathic Parkinson's disease (IPD) or with a related Parkinsonism such as Progressive Supranuclear Palsy (PSP), Multisystem Atrophy (MSA), Cortical Basal Degeneration (CBD), nor does the metadata specify whether a participant's IPD or Parkinsonism is currently being treated using Deep Brain Stimulation (DBS) or levodopa. Using data from SAP, it has been reported that one can reduce ASR error rates by 35% for one group of speakers with Parkinson's (the SAP dev and test sets) by training the ASR using speech from another group with Parkinson's (the SAP training set) [24], and that the error rate of a commercial ASR can be reduced by factors between 20% and 65% for different etiologies of speech disorder [25]. Competitors in a challenge competition using these data[1] successfully reduced ASR error rate by a factor of three relative to the best open-source ASR. Researchers using the data to improve their speech technologies include members of the AI Accessibility Coalition (the University of Illinois, Amazon, Apple, Google, Meta, and Microsoft), and 54 other universities and companies by the end of 2024. Among these organizations, several have expressed goals that include scientific analyses and clinical development for the benefit of people with Parkinson's disease.

This article provides descriptive reports on speech pattern variability observed in a subset of the SAP dataset, specifically from people with Parkinson's disease. Section 2 provides example spectrograms and acoustic measurements characterizing both intonational dysprosody (monopitch) and rhythmic dysprosody (large variations in speaking rate). Section 3 provides example spectrograms and acoustic measurements characterizing dysphonia, including hoarse, breathy, and aphonic productions. Section 4 provides example spectrograms and acoustic measurements characterizing articulatory disorders including both reduced articulation and excessive stuttering. Section 5 discusses the frequencies with which these different speech patterns occur in the SAP corpus, as measured based on perceptual measurements of the differential diagnostic patterns of dysarthria [26], and the high degree of within-subject variability observed due to fatigue and performance effects. Section 6 concludes.

[1] https://eval.ai/web/challenges/challenge-page/2362/overview.

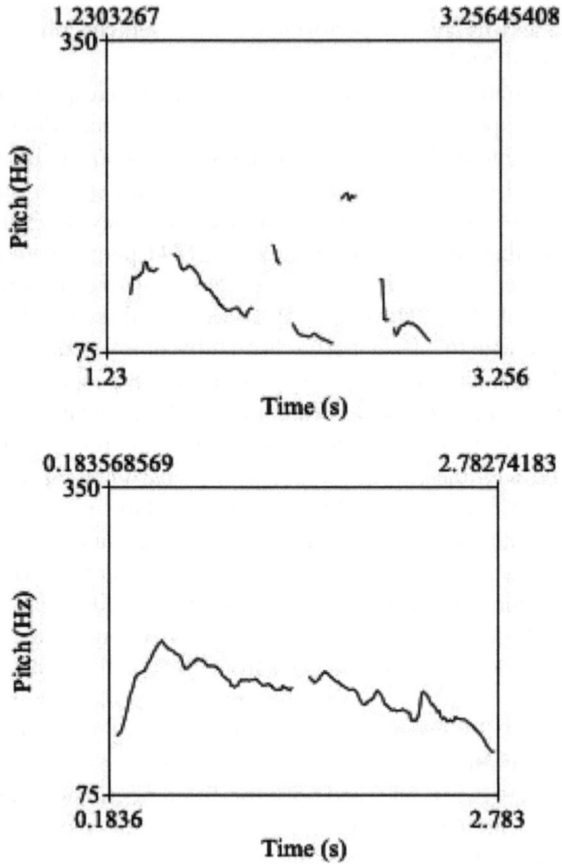

Fig. 1. Pitch contour of the same utterance produced by (a) an individual with PD whose perceptual ratings indicate high intelligibility and (b) one with PD whose perceptual ratings indicate moderate intelligibility. The pitch contour was extracted using the Praat software. Utterance text: "What's on my calendar tomorrow?".

2 Examples of Intonational and Rhythmic Dysprosody

Prosodic correlates of Parkinson's disease include a flattened intonational contour, and highly variable rhythmic patterns that may include very slow speaking rate, very high speaking rate, and atypical pause locations.

The characteristic intonational contour of Parkinson's disease has been called "monopitch" [13], which is an allusion to perceptual similarities, reported early in the history of speech analysis, between the speech typical of Parkinson's disease and other types of speech disorders characterized by monotonic fundamental frequency [27]. People without neurodegenerative diseases may use flat intonation for social reasons including casual conversation or boredom, e.g., utterances in the Switchboard corpus of conversational speech have fewer than half as many pitch excursions as do utterances in the Boston University Radio Speech corpus [28]. There may be a relationship between the monopitch of Parkinson's disease and the monopitch of boredom, e.g., one study [29] found that people with Parkinson's disease showed reduced perceptual ability to detect the acoustic correlates of emotion in the speech of others. It has been reported that trained listeners are able to distinguish the flat intonations of Parkinson's disease from the flat intonations indicative of boredom [30], but the acoustic features that make this distinction possible are unclear: one early study of a single post-encephalitic patient with PD reported very high pitch range [12] as compared to the low pitch range typical of boredom [31], but the report of high pitch range in Parkinson's has not been confirmed in any larger population study. Automatic voice analysis systems are able to detect the acoustic correlates of Parkinson's disease with relatively high specificity and sensitivity, although a recent review noted that published methods rarely show cross-corpus generalization accuracy that is comparably high with the accuracy of a system whose training and testing data were collected using matching prompts and microphones [32].

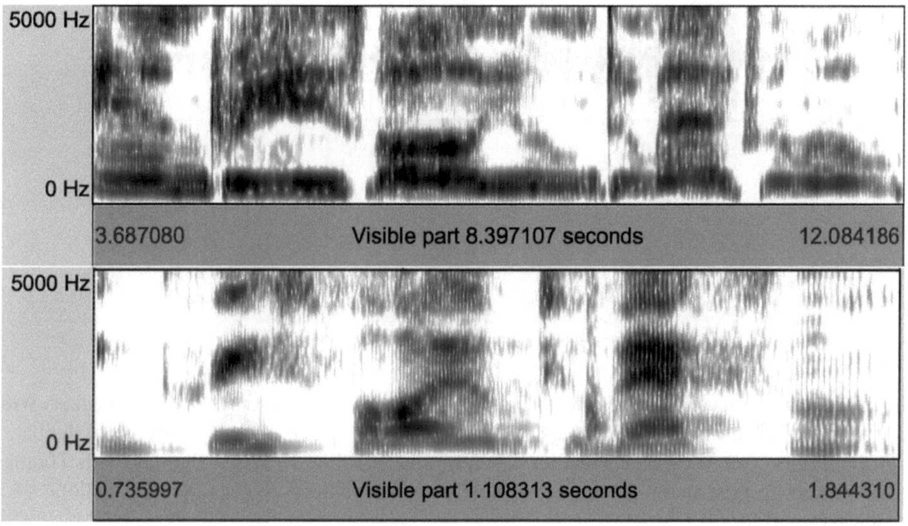

Fig. 2. Spectrogram of the same utterance produced by two speakers with Parkinson's disease. Utterance text: "Increase volume to maximum." Notice the difference in time scales: The top speaker spends 8.4 s producing this utterance, while the bottom speakers spends 1.1 s.

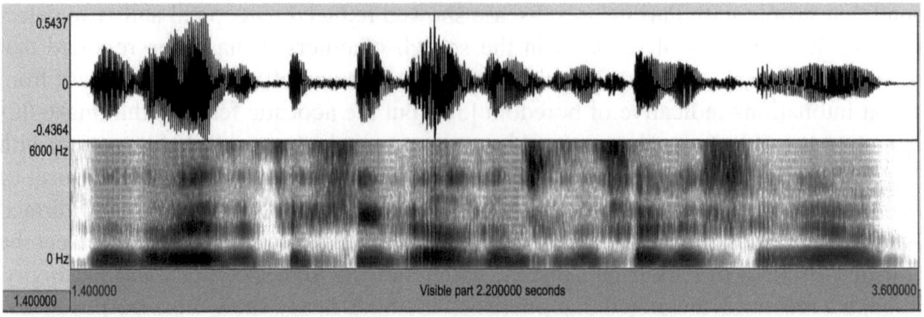

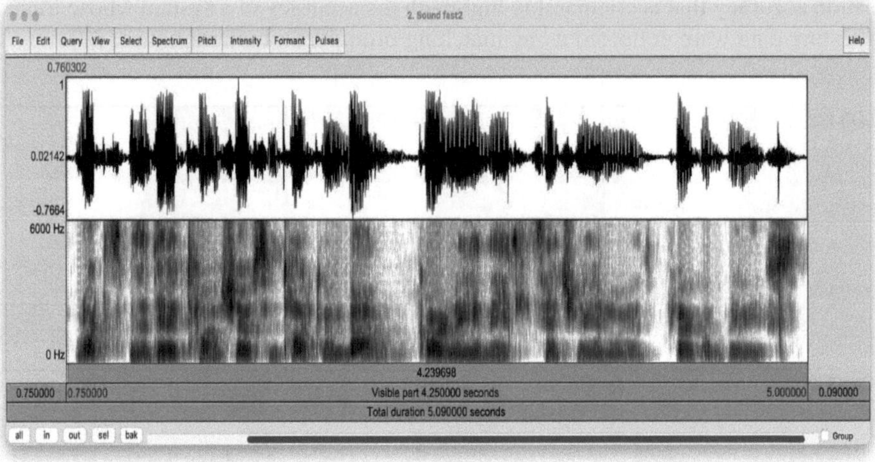

Fig. 3. Spectrograms of two utterances with very high speaking rates, produced by speakers with Parkinson's disease in the SAP corpus. Utterance texts: "That is the way they keep elephants with the circus, you know" (7 syllables/second), and "I'd like to spend the day with Thomas Jefferson, talk to him about gardening in the eighteenth century and his political beliefs" (8.3 syllables/second).

Figure 1 shows the f0 contour of an utterance produced by an individual with high intelligibility vs. an individual with moderate intelligibility. The speaker with high intelligibility produced strong pitch accents on the words "calendar" and "tomorrow," visible as discontinuous peaks in the pitch contour with peak-to-valley excursion amplitude of approximately 100Hz. The speaker with moderate intelligibility has pitch accents on the same two words, but with much lower peak-to-valley excursion amplitude. Both speakers produced this phrase using a single intonational phrase, using a phrasal pitch contour with approximately 90 Hz peak-to-valley amplitude, but the speaker with high intelligibility produced a phrase contour that drops off quickly from its peak toward a valley in the penultimate word of the utterance ("calendar"), while the speaker with moderate intelligibility produced a phrase contour that drops off more gradually from its peak toward a valley at the very end of the last word of the utterance ("tomorrow").

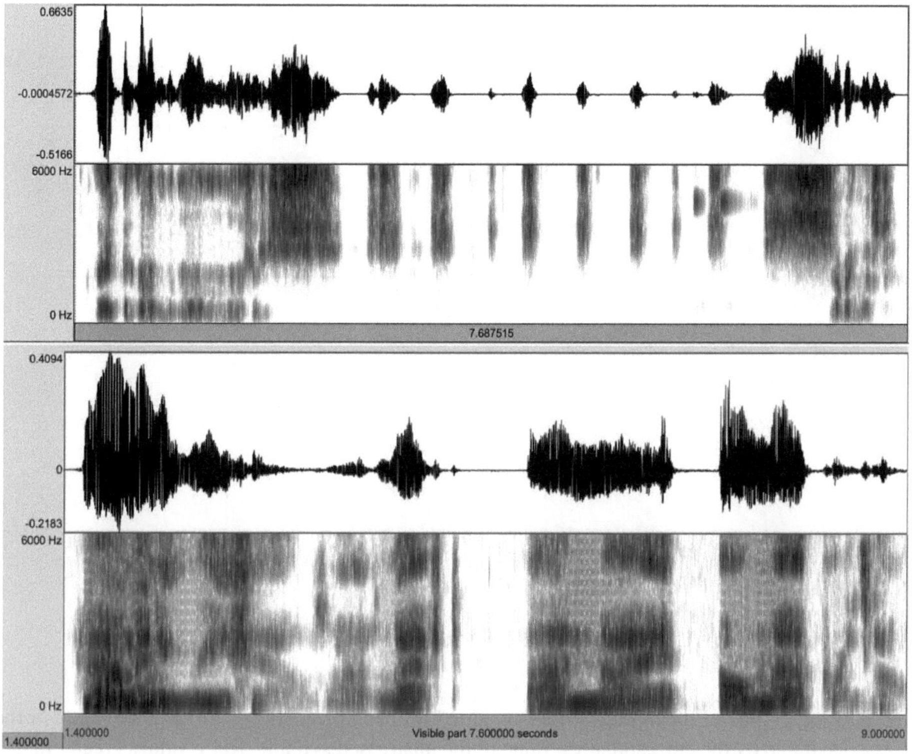

Fig. 4. Spectrogram of two utterances with very low speaking rates, produced by speakers with Parkinson's disease in the SAP corpus. Utterance texts: "Set a reminder to take…" (one syllable per second), "How many refills are left on my Omeprazole?" (1.7 syllables/second).

Another prosodic characteristics in hypokinetic dysarthria is durational abnormality. While the average speaking rate of people with Parkinson's disease is not significantly different from that of people without disorder [33, 34], fast speaking rates or short rushes of speech are described as a distinct feature in hypokinetic dysarthria [35, 36].

On the other hand, a slower than normal rate is reported, often associated with prolongations of segments and/or longer pause duration. Studies together suggest variable speaking rates across speakers [26, 37]. Such variability across IPD and Parkinsonisms in the SAP corpus is considerable. Figure 2 shows spectrograms of two speakers reading the same utterance, one (top) with an extremely low speaking rate (less than one syllable per second) and one (bottom) with an extremely high speaking rate (more than 7 syllables per second). Additional examples are provided in Fig. 3 and Fig. 4. Figure 3 shows spectrograms of two speakers with extremely high speaking rates (more than 7 syllables per second). Figure 4 shows spectrograms of two speakers with extremely low speaking rates: less than one syllable per second.

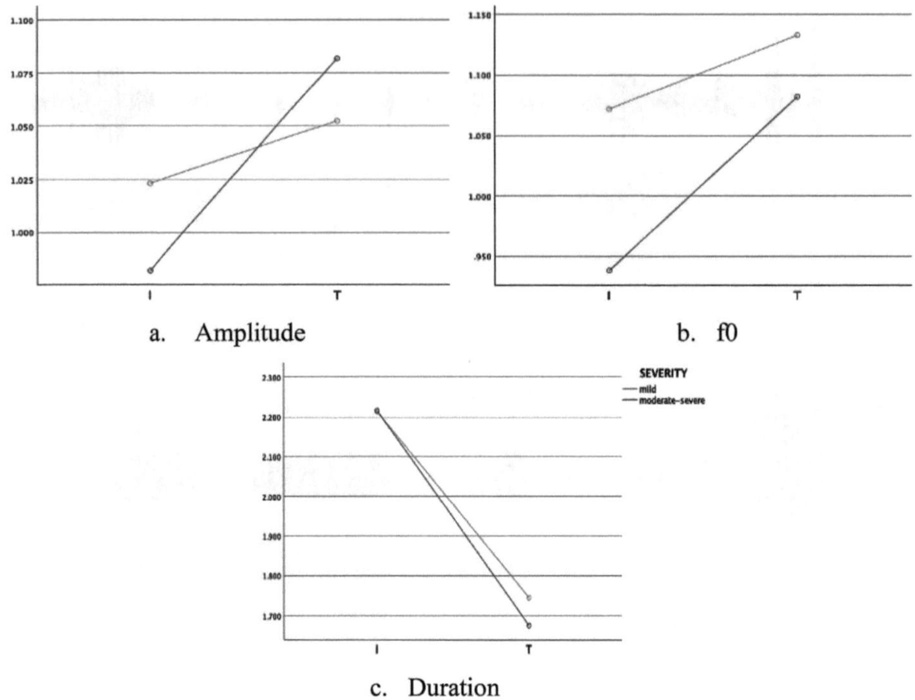

Fig. 5. Line graphs of mean ratio values obtained for each measure by dividing the value of the stressed syllable by the corresponding value of the unstressed syllable. Ratio values greater than 1 indicate a degree of prominence in the stressed syllable. I and T denote iambic and trochaic stress patterns (iambic: unstressed syllable followed by stressed, trochaic: stressed syllable followed by unstressed).

Prosodic features such as loudness, pitch and duration mark lexical stress which plays a critical role in English, by disambiguating word meaning and enhancing word recognition. Our preliminary analyses of acoustic features of lexical stress in 10 speakers with PD in the SAP data examined lexical stress as a function of stress location in words and severity [38]. Figure 5 shows mean value ratios of amplitude, f0, and duration between stressed and unstressed syllables. In each plot, the numbers shown at left (axis label: "I") show the ratio of stressed over unstressed syllable in iambic bisyllable patterns (unstressed syllable followed by stressed), while the numbers shown at right (axis label: "T") show the ratio of stressed over unstressed syllable in trochaic bisyllable patterns (stressed syllable followed by unstressed). As shown, speakers with high intelligibility (mild group) exhibit greater amplitude and f0 in stressed than unstressed syllables (ratio greater than 1.0) in both iambic and trochaic stress patterns, while speakers with moderate-severe intelligibility show this pattern only in trochaic stress patterns. That is, as the disease progresses, monoloudness and monopitch become more pronounced, especially for iambic words. Duration patterns differently. All speakers (both mild and moderate-severe groups) show greater duration on the stressed syllable in both trochaic and iambic stress patterns, with a greater effect observed in iambic patterns. In addition, durational ratios exceed amplitude and f0 ratios for both speaker groups and for both trochaic and iambic words, suggesting that duration is consistently the strongest cue for marking lexical stress.

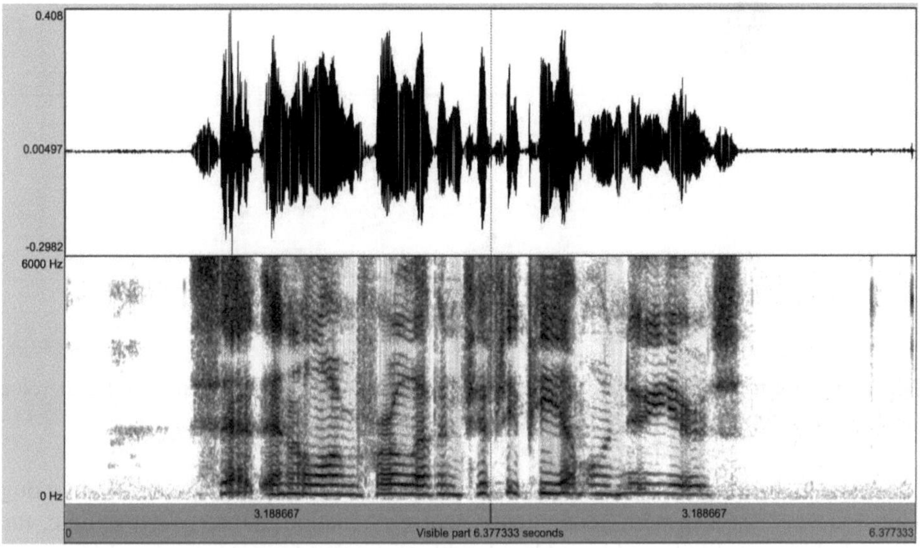

Fig. 6. Waveform and narrowband spectrogram of an utterance with perceptually breathy voice quality. Frequency scale for spectrogram shown at left. Text: "Set an alarm for 11:50 PM on New Year's Eve.

3 Examples of Hoarse, Breathy and Aphonic Dysphonia

Breathy, harsh, and aphonic voice are typical of hypokinetic dysarthria due to laryngeal dysfunction [39]. Figure 6 shows an example of a waveform and narrowband spectrogram of an utterance with perceptually breathy voice quality. Notice the high degree of aspiration noise between harmonics of the fundamental frequency. In the first two syllables, in particular, only three or four harmonics are visible; all higher harmonics are masked by aspiration. Figure 7, by contrast, shows the waveform and spectrogram of an utterance with perceptually harsh voice quality. Published acoustic studies of harsh voice quality associate it with nonlinear voicing phenomena such as diplophonia (the presence of spectral energy at harmonics of half the pitch frequency) [17]. The sample shown in Fig. 7 does not show evidence of diplophonia, but it shows evidence of spectral flattening: all harmonics of the fundamental frequency have nearly uniform magnitude, between the first harmonic at 269Hz and the twenty-third harmonic at nearly 6000Hz. Spectral flattening has not been reported as a correlate of harsh voice, but has been reported as a correlate of pressed voice [40], which is a term used as a synonym for harsh voice in some published studies [41]. The speaker's impaired voice control is also responsible for the very loud first syllable, which has a waveform magnitude almost four times larger than the magnitude of the remaining syllables.

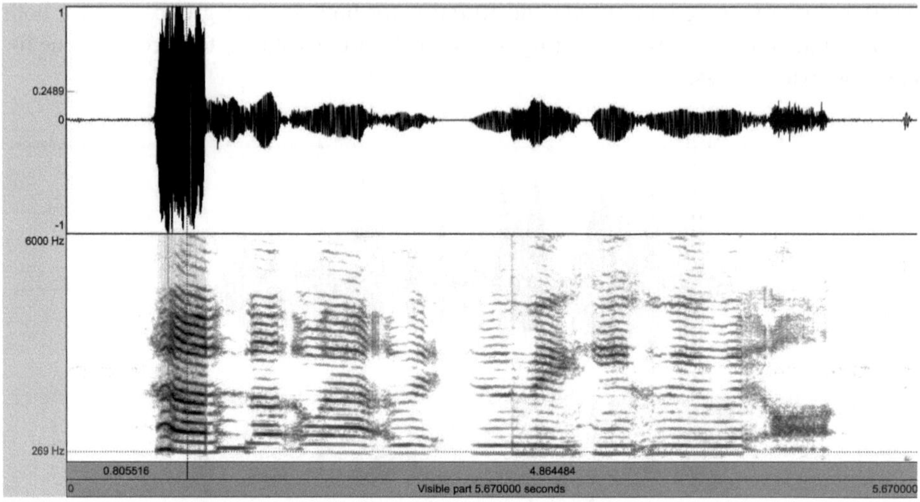

Fig. 7. Waveform and narrowband spectrogram of an utterance with perceptually harsh voice quality. Text: "How's the traffic at the St. Louis Arch?"

Figure 8 is the spectrogram of the utterance "One of my pet peeves is when a dog jumps on you," spoken with perceptually hoarse phonation. Notice, for example, the relatively high amplitude and broad bandwidth of the first formant (the band of energy below 1000 Hz in the spectrogram). Notice also the glottal stop at closure of the /t/ in "pet" (end of the fourth syllable, end of the third sonorant segment), preceded by three irregularly spaced glottal closure events that correlate with a sudden increase in the detected f0. Similarly, the end of the word "is" (sixth syllable, fifth sonorant segment, center of the window shown) exhibits a kind of strangled voicing, with substantial decrease in energy at the end of the vowel (tracked by a halving of the apparent f0) followed by a sudden increase in energy at start of the consonant.

In extreme cases, the phonatory effort of a person with Parkinson's disease may be reduced so far that phonation ceases entirely, resulting in speech that is essentially aphonic or whispered (Fig. 9). Notice the complete absence of any visible spectral energy below the first formant, and the near absence of first-formant energy: the first formant is only visible in the spectrogram during the /u/ of "snooze," and again during the /l/ and second syllable of the word "alarm."

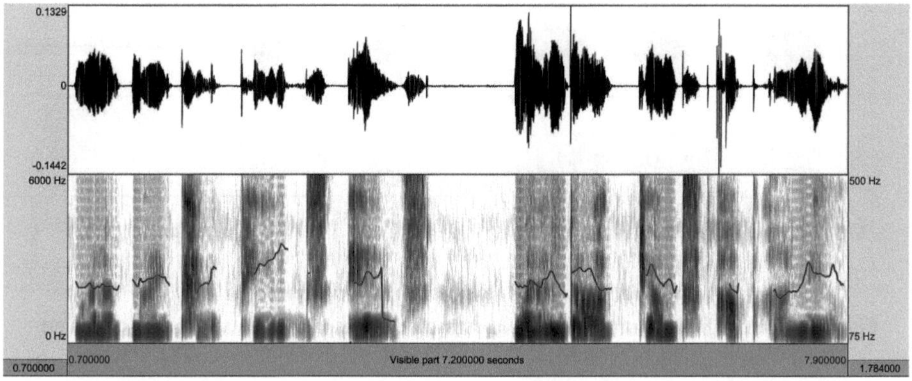

Fig. 8. Broadband spectrogram and pitch contour of an utterance with perceptually hoarse voice quality. Frequency scale for spectrogram shown at left, frequency scale for pitch shown at right. Text: "One of my pet peeves is when a dog jumps on you."

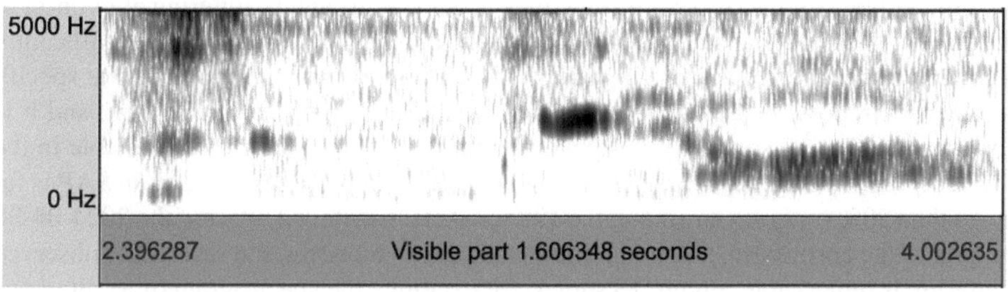

Fig. 9. Spectrogram of an utterance with no modally voiced vowels produced by a speaker with Parkinson's disease. Utterance text: "Snooze the alarm." Audio was recorded without calibrated sound pressure levels, but it is noteworthy that this speaker's utterances are at lower recording levels than those of speakers with modally voiced vowels.

4 Examples of Dysarthria and Stuttering

Imprecise articulation comprises a prominent speech pattern in hypokinetic dysarthria, such as spirantization of stop consonants [37, 42]. Figure 10 shows voicing errors observed in the SAP data. In the production of the utterance "they don't have the guts", devoicing of /d/ and /g/ is evident, as demonstrated by the degree of aspiration or the long duration between the release of the consonant and the onset of voicing.

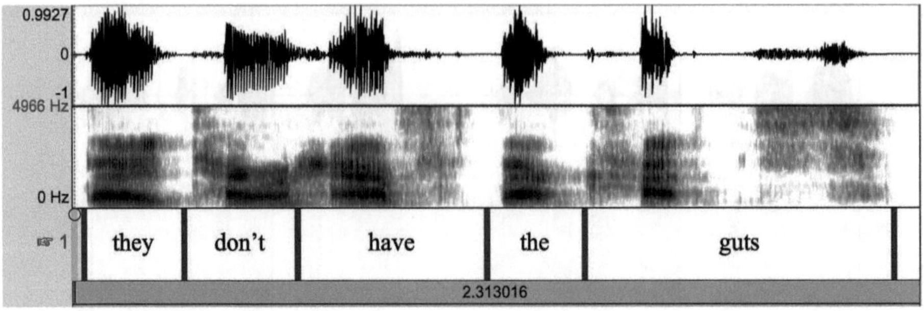

Fig. 10. Spectrogram of an utterance where voiced consonants /d/ and /g/ are devoiced.

Figure 11 illustrates an example of a consonant cluster becoming a singleton. In the utterance "divided up into couples", the final consonant cluster /lz/ is produced as [z]. In addition, both Fig. 11 and Fig. 12 provide examples of deletion of unstressed syllables: [pə] in "couples" and [ri] in "Carey", respectively. It has been reported that as many as 20% of people with Parkinson's disease may acquire neurogenic stuttering after onset of the disease [43], and that stuttering-like disfluency in Parkinson's disease is significantly increased under the influence of levodopa [44]. These published reports do not specify whether the reported cases were associated with IPD or with Parkinsonisms, and it is also impossible to distinguish these two possible etiologies using data available in the SAP corpus. The number of people with severe stuttering-like disfluencies in SAP is far fewer than 20% (only seven among the 428 speakers distributed s part of the 2024-04-30 version of the corpus [45]). Among those who stutter, however, the severity of observed stuttering is remarkable. Figure 13 shows, for example, the spectrogram of an utterance in which the first syllable of the word "shopping" is repeated twenty times.

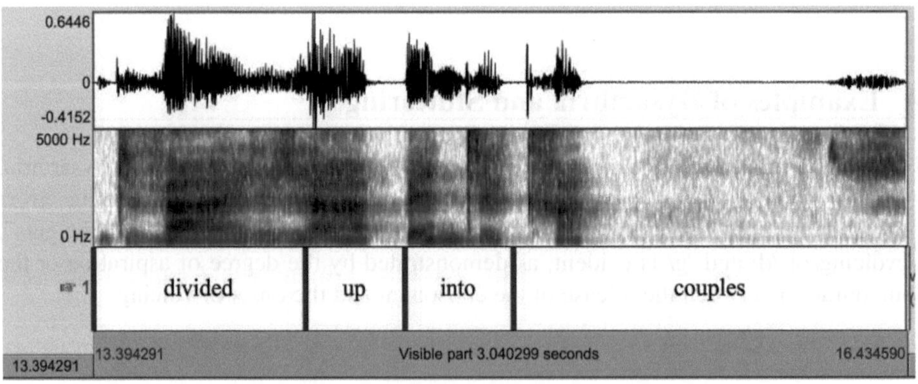

Fig. 11. Spectrogram of an utterance where [ˈkʌpəlz] is spoken as [ˈkʌz].

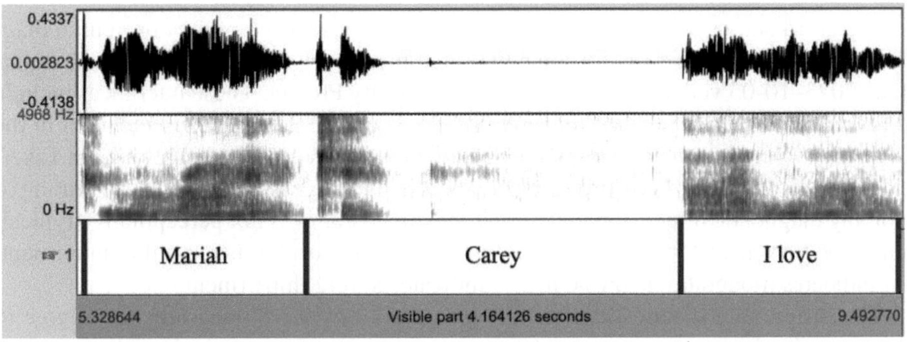

Fig. 12. Spectrogram of an utterance where the second syllable [ri] in'Carey' is deleted.

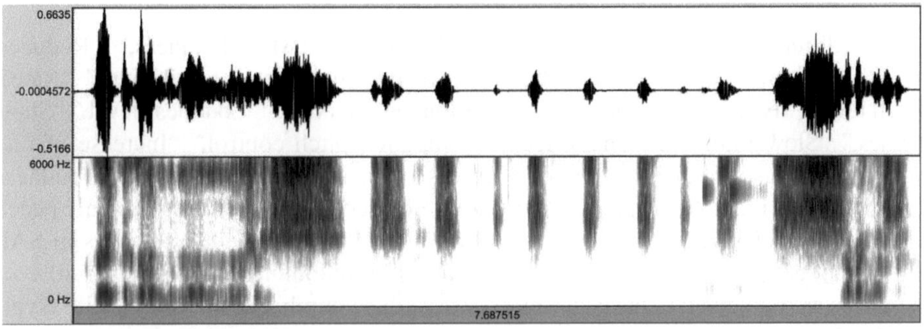

Fig. 13. People with IPD or Parkinsonisms may exhibit extremely high rates of stuttering-like disfluency. In this example ("Create a grocery shopping list"), the first syllable of the word "grocery" is repeated seven times, while the first syllable of the word "shopping" is repeated twenty times.

5 Inter-speaker and Intra-speaker Variation in the Perceptual Correlates of Parkinson's Disease

In order to facilitate exploration and analysis of SAP data, up to thirty speech recordings per talker have been annotated using perceptual scales based on the differential diagnostic patterns of dysarthria [35]. All such recordings were annotated by certified speech-language pathologists who have been trained in the use of the differential diagnostic patterns. Annotators listened to speech samples using headphones, by playing the waveforms at the same loudness (SPL) level, using a custom-developed web application. Because of the very large scale of this operation, formal inter-annotator agreement statistics were not collected, but all annotators were trained together in a full-semester course on motor speech disorders taught by the second author, received additional training when they started the project, and consult one another frequently by e-mail or in person to discuss difficult cases. The distributions of these patterns provide information about the frequency with which different types of dysprosody, dysphonia, and dysarthria are observed in the SAP corpus.

Figure 14 shows the distribution of atypical ratings, on each of the differential diagnostic patterns of dysarthria, for the 6405 rated utterances that were distributed as part of the 2023–10-05 version of the Speech Accessibility Project. These utterances include up to thirty utterances per speaker (average: 25.3) for the 253 speakers included in the 2023–10-05 version of the corpus. Each utterance is rated on up to 42 distinct Likert scales, producing up to 42 distinct integer labels in the range between 1 and 7. A rating of 1 for any diagnostic dimension means that the dimension was not perceptually atypical; ratings of 1 are therefore not shown in Fig. 14. Ratings of 2 indicate mild impairment, 3–4 indicates moderate impairment, 5–7 indicates severe impairment.

The differential diagnostic pattern "Naturalness (overall)" measures the degree to which a trained listener perceives the speech to deviate from typical productions. As shown in Fig. 14, almost all rated utterances in SAP deviate from typical speech in some way, with the majority of utterances rated to have moderate impairment (ratings of 3 or 4).

The differential diagnostic patterns "Monopitch," "Monoloudness," "Reduced stress," "Variable rate," "Short rushes of speech," "Inappropriate silences," "Rate," "Pitch level," "Excess and equal stress," "Prolonged intervals," "Loudness level," "Short phrases," "Slow rate," "Loudness decay," "Impaired pitch control," "Increase of rate overall," "Increase of rate in segments," "Excess loudness variation," "Impaired loudness control," and "Impaired emphasis" measure perceived deviations from typical speech prosody (dysprosody; Sect. 2). As shown in Fig. 14, a majority of utterances in SAP exhibit moderate degrees of "Mono pitch" and "Monoloudness." More than 40% of utterances are perceived to have "Reduced stress." The number of utterances with atypical "Rate" (consistently fast or consistently slow) is roughly 10%, while the number with "Variable rate" is roughly 20%. Other types of dysprosody occur in 10% of utterances or fewer.

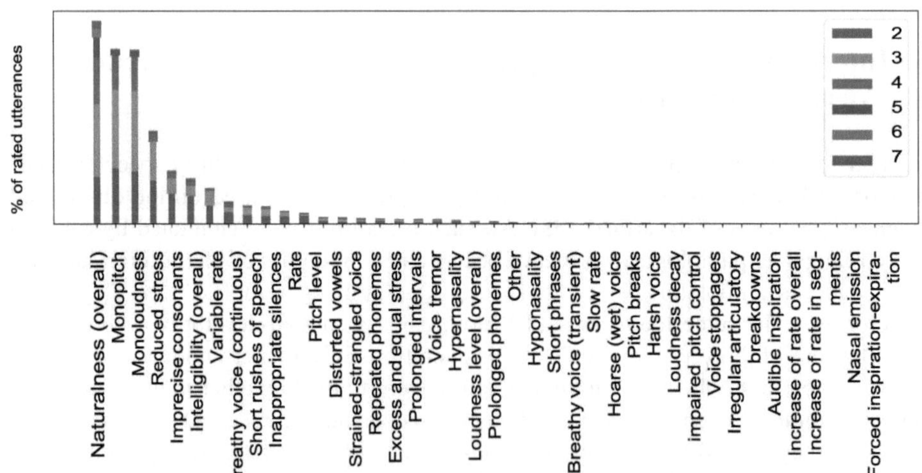

Fig. 14. Distribution of utterances rated as atypical on each of the differential diagnostic patterns of dysarthria by trained raters. Utterances within normal limits are rated 1 (not shown), utterances with mild impairment are rated 2, moderate impairment is 3 or 4, severe impairment is 5, 6, or 7.

The differential diagnostic patterns "Breathy voice (continuous)," "Strained-strangled voice," "Hypernasality," "Breathy voice (transient)," "Voice tremor," "Hoarse (wet) voice," and "Harsh voice" measure perceived deviations from typical voicing (dysphonia; Sect. 3). As shown in Fig. 14, only about 15% of speech samples in SAP 2023-10-05 are atypically breathy, and the number of samples exhibiting hoarseness or tremor is smaller than 15%.

Dysarthria may be defined to be a loss of intelligibility caused by neuromotor disorder [26]; the presence of perceptible dysarthria in a speech sample is measured by the differential diagnostic pattern "Intelligibility (overall)." The differential diagnostic patterns "Imprecise consonants" and "Intelligibility (overall)" are both perceptually atypical in about 20% of SAP 2023-10-05. Ratings on these two diagnostic dimensions are highly correlated ($r = 0.90$, $p < 1.7e\ 80$): most utterances with atypical intelligibility have atypical consonant productions, and vice versa. Other possible sources of intelligibility loss, such as "Distorted vowels," "Hyponasality," and "Irregular articulatory breakdowns," are considered relatively uncommon for PD, and occur with low frequency among speakers with PD in the SAP corpus.

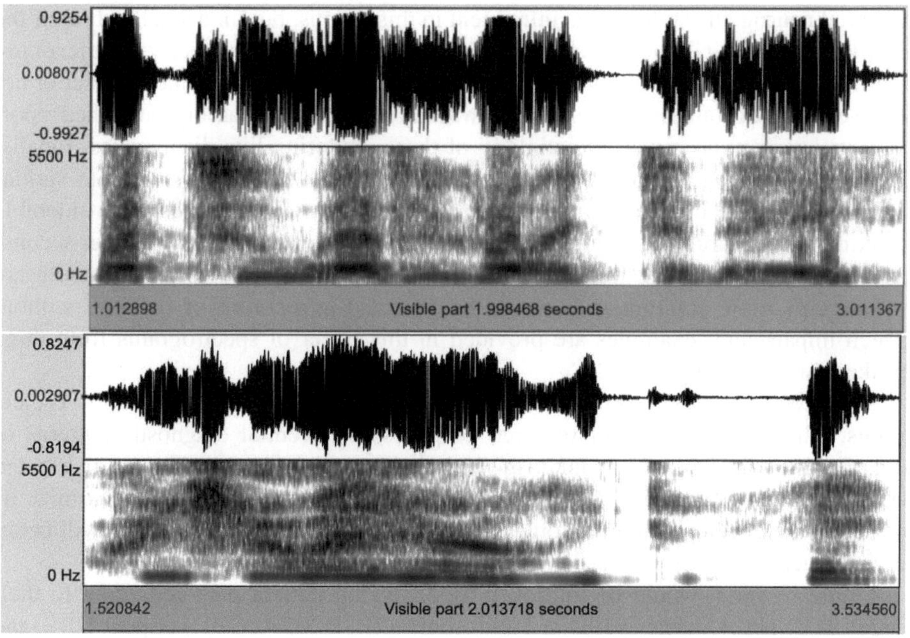

Fig. 15. Spectrogram of two productions of the text "What's the weather like today?" by the same speaker at different times of the day, 4 h apart

The differential diagnostic pattern "Repeated phonemes" and "Prolonged phonemes" measure the perceived degree of stuttering-like repetition and prolongation of phonemes, syllables, and words. Stuttering is an unusual attribute of utterances in SAP 2023–10-05, occurring in fewer than 5% of all rated utterances. These utterances are not uniformly distributed. There are seven speakers who stutter approximately fifty percent of their utterances, while the remaining 246 speakers rarely exhibit stuttering-like disfluencies. Because the distinction between IPD and Parkinsonisms is not specified in SAP metadata, it is not possible using SAP data to determine whether stuttering is associated with IPD or with a related diagnosis; examples provided in the published literature are similarly ambiguous [43].

Speakers are encouraged to record at different times of day so that the SAP data captures intra-speaker variations over time. Figure 15 shows two productions of the same text, spoken by the same speaker at different times of the day. The second example illustrates the effect of fatigue, evident by the diffused harmonics and the lack of modal phonation in some syllables.

6 Conclusions

The Speech Accessibility Project (SAP) provides a unique opportunity for a broad-ranging survey of speech patterns that may be symptomatic of Parkinson's disease. Most speakers in the corpus exhibit classic patterns of hypokinetic dysarthria, including reduced loudness, monopitch, monoloudness, breathy voice, and reduced articulation. Acquired neurogenic stuttering is infrequent in this corpus, but for a small subset of the recorded speakers, it is quite severe; because the metadata does not specify whether or not a participant is currently taking levodopa, it is not possible to determine whether or not observed cases of stuttering are associated with levodopa, but at least one published report suggests levodopa as a possible etiology of these stuttering-like disfluencies. Finally, although the average speaking rate of participants with Parkinson's is quite similar to the average rate of speakers without Parkinson's, that average masks considerable speaking rate variability, from less than one to greater than seven syllables per second. Very slow speech is more frequent than very fast speech in this corpus, but both are considerably more common than would be expected in a corpus of speakers without speech impairment; examples are provided in this paper of spectrograms from three speakers in each group.

All speech samples shown in this paper are part of the Speech Accessibility Project corpus, which is available for research purposes. Differential diagnostic patterns of dysarthria, rated by speech and language pathologists trained in their use, are distributed with the corpus. The variety and volume of this corpus are designed to maximize its impact on the development of automatic speech recognition technology that will better serve the needs of people with Parkinson's disease.

Future research would be improved by analyzing patient data according to their diagnosis by neurologists as IPD or Parkinsonism (PSP, MSA, CBD) or post-DBS, and by their levodopa treatment status (currently taking vs. not taking levodopa). These metadata are not provided with SAP as a measure intended to protect patient privacy in this widely distributed research corpus, but smaller datasets collected with relevant metadata might help to shed light on the etiology of each of the patterns of speech reported in this paper.

References

1. Limousin, P., Foltynie, T.: Long-term outcomes of deep brain stimulation in parkinson disease. Nat. Rev. Neurol. **15**(4), 234–242 (2019)
2. LeWitt, P.A., Fahn, S.: Levodopa therapy for Parkinson disease: a look backward and forward. Neurology **86**(14_supplement_1), S3–S12 (2016)
3. Ramig, L., Halpern, A., Spielman, J., Fox, C., Freeman, K.: Speech treatment in parkinson's disease: Randomized control trial. Mov. Disord. **33**(11), 1777–1791 (2018)
4. Daoudi, K., Das, B., Tykalova, T., Klempir, J., Rusz, J.: Speech acoustic indices for differential diagnosis between parkinson's disease, multiple system atrophy and progressive supranuclear palsy. npj Parkinson's Dis. **8**(1), 142 (2022)
5. Vaillancourt, D.E., et al.: Automated imaging differentiation for parkinsonism. JAMA Neurol. **82**, E1–E10 (2025)
6. Tsuboi, T., et al.: Distinct phenotypes of speech and voice disorders in parkinson's disease after subthalamic nucleus deep brain stimulation. J. Neurol. Neurosurg. Psychiatry **86**(8), 856–864 (2015)
7. Hasegawa-Johnson, M., et al.: Community-supported shared infrastructure in support of speech accessibility. J. Speech Lang. Hear. Res. **67**(10), 4162–4175 (2024)
8. Geng, M., et al.: Use of speech impairment severity for dysarthric speech recognition. In: Proceedings of Interspeech, ISCA, 2023, pp. 2328–2332 (2023)
9. Moro-Velazquez, L., et al.: Study of the performance of automatic speech recognition systems in speakers with parkinson's disease. In: Proceedings of Interspeech 2019, pp. 3875–3879 (2019)
10. Parkinson, J.: An Essay on the Shaking Palsy. Whitingham and Rowland, London (1817)
11. Ardran, G., Kinsbourne, M., Rushworth, G.: Dysphonia due to tremor. J. Neurol. Neurosurg. Psychiatry **29**(3), 219 (1966)
12. Grewel, F.: Dysarthria in post-encephalitic parkinsonism. Acta Psychiatr. Scand. **32**(4), 440–449 (1957)
13. Aronson, A.E., Brown, J.R., Litin, E.M., Pearson, J.S.: Spastic dysphonia. ii. Comparison with essential (voice) tremor and other neurologic and psychogenic dysphonias. J. Speech Hear. Disord. **33**(3), 219–231 (1968)
14. Canter, G.J.: Speech characteristics of patients with parkinson's disease: 3. articulation, diadochokinesis, and over-all speech adequacy. J. Speech Hear. Disord. **30**(3), 217–224 (1965)
15. Tikofsky, R.S., Tikofsky, R.P.: Intelligibility measures of dysarthric speech. J. Speech Hear. Res. **7**(4), 325–333 (1964)
16. Tu, M., Wisler, A., Berisha, V., Liss, J.M.: The relationship between perceptual disturbances in dysarthric speech and automatic speech recognition performance. J. Acoust. Soc. Am. **140**(5), EL416–EL422 (2016)
17. Aminoff, M., Dedo, H., Izdebski, K.: Clinical aspects of spasmodic dysphonia. J. Neurol. Neurosurg. Psychiat. **41**(4), 361–365 (1978)
18. Muhammad, G., Mesallam, T.A., Malki, K.H., Farahat, M., Alsulaiman, M., Bukhari, M.: Formant analysis in dysphonic patients and automatic arabic digit speech recognition. Biomed. Eng. Online **10**, 1–12 (2011)
19. Levy, E.S., et al.: LANCET EClinicalMedicine **24** (2020)
20. Whitty, C.: Cortical dysarthria and dysprosody of speech. J. Neurol. Neurosurg. Psychiatry **27**(6), 507 (1964)
21. Godfrey, J., Holliman, E., McDaniel, J.: SWITCHBOARD: telephone speech corpus for research and development. In: Proceedings of ICASSP, San Francisco, pp. 517–520 (1992)
22. Panayotov, V., Chen, G., Povey, D., Khudanpur, S.: Librispeech: an asr corpus based on public domain audio books. In: 2015 IEEE International Conference on Acoustics, Speech and Signal Processing (ICASSP), pp. 5206–5210. IEEE (2015)

23. Kim, H., et al.: Dysarthric speech database for universal access research. In: Proceedings of Interspeech, pp. 1741–1744 (2008)
24. Zheng, X., Phukon, B., Hasegawa-Johnson, M.: Fine-tuning automatic speech recognition for people with parkinson's: an effective strategy for enhancing speech technology accessibility. In: Proceedings of Interspeech, vol. 9 (2024)
25. HeikoRa. Latest updates to the azure ai speech service. In: Azure AI Services Blog (2024). https://techcommunity.microsoft.com/blog/azure-ai-services-blog/latest-updates-to-the-azure-ai-speech-service/4300129
26. Darley, F., Aronson, A.: Motor Speech Disorders. W.B. Saunders Co., Philadelphia (1975)
27. McGrew, J.F.: Correcting defects of the speaking voice. Western Speech **12**(3) (1948)
28. Chavarria, S., Yoon, T., Cole, J., Hasegawa-Johnson, M.: Acoustic differentiation of ip and IP boundary levels: comparison of land L-L% in the switchboard corpus. In: Proceedings of Speech Prosody, Nara, Japan (2004)
29. Kwan, L.C., Whitehill, T.L.: Perception of speech by individuals with parkinson's disease: a review. Parkinson's Dis. **2011**(1), 389767 (2011)
30. Miller, N.: Communication changes in parkinson's disease. Pract. Neurol. **17**(4), 266–274 (2017)
31. Zhang, T., Hasegawa-Johnson, M., Levinson, S.E.: Cognitive state classification in a spoken tutorial dialogue system. Speech Commun. **48**(6), 616–632 (2006)
32. Moro-Velazquez, L., Gomez-Garcia, J.A., Arias-Londoño, J.D., Dehak, N., Godino-Llorente, J.I.: Advances in parkinson's disease detection and assessment using voice and speech: a review of the articulatory and phonatory aspects. Biomed. Signal Process. Control **66**, 102418 (2021)
33. Caligiuri, M.P.: The influence of speaking rate on articulatory hypokinesia in parkinsonian dysarthria. Brain Lang. **36**(3), 493–502 (1989)
34. Skodda, S., Schlegel, U.: Speech rate and rhythm in parkinson's disease. Mov. Disord. Off. J. Mov. Disord. Soc. **23**(7), 985–992 (2008)
35. Darley, F.L., Aronson, A.E., Brown, J.R.: Differential diagnostic patterns of dysarthria. J. Speech Hear. Res. **12**, 246–269 (1969)
36. Liss, J., et al.: Quantifying speech rhythm abnormalities in the dysarthrias. J. Speech Lang. Hear. Res. **52**(5), 1334–1352 (2009)
37. Weismer, G.: Articulatory Characteristics of Parkinsonian Dysarthria, pp. 101–130. College-Hill Press (1984)
38. Penrod, C., Kim, H.: Comparison of acoustic features of lexical stress in dysarthric speech. In: Illinois Speech Language Hearing Association Annual Convention (2025)
39. Smith, M., Ramig, L., Perez, K., Samandari, R.: Intensive voice treatment in Parkinson disease: laryngostroboscopic findings. J. Voice **9**, 453–459 (1995)
40. Ishi, C., Ishiguro, H., Hagita, N.: Acoustic analysis of pressed voice. J. Acoust. Soc. Ame. **120**(5_Supplement), 3374– 3374 (2006)
41. Moisik, S.R.: Harsh voice quality and its association with blackness in popular American media. Phonetica **69**(4), 193–215 (2013)
42. Kent, R.D., Weismer, G., Kent, J., Rosenbek, J.: Toward phonetic intelligibility testing in dysarthria. J. Speech Hear. Disord. **54**(4), 482–499 (1984)
43. Gooch, E.A., et al.: Acquired stuttering in parkinson's disease. Mov. Disord. Clin. Pract. **10**(6), 956–966 (2023)
44. Im, H., Adams, S., Abeyesekera, A., Pieterman, M., Gilmore, G., Jog, M.: Effect of levodopa on speech dysfluency in parkinson's disease. Mov. Disord. Clin. Pract. **6**(2), 150–154 (2019)
45. Na, J., Zheng, X., Hasegawa-Johnson, M., Lee, B.: Improved recognition of the speech of people with parkinson's who stutter. In: Proceedings of ICASSP (2025)

A Survey of Open Voice and Speech Datasets for the Screening and Evaluation of Parkinson's Disease

Juan C. Puerta-Acevedo(✉), Maria F. Alcalá-Durand, Julián D. Arias-Londoño, and Juan I. Godino-Llorente

ETSI Telecomunicación, Universidad Politécnica de Madrid, 28040 Madrid, Spain
juancamilo.puerta@upm.es

Abstract. In recent years, a growing number of corpora have been created for the analysis of the speech uttered by patients with Parkinson's disease, yet only a fraction are openly accessible to the research community. This paper presents a systematic review and comparative analysis of all known publicly available speech corpora developed for this purpose, regardless of language or collection context.

The study identifies ten datasets, which are individually evaluated across five key dimensions: (1) demographics and size; (2) recording protocols and quality; (3) speech task types; (4) accessibility and licensing; and (5) availability of raw audio and/or acoustic features.

The evaluation reveals considerable variability in recording conditions, task diversity, metadata richness, and openness. Some datasets prioritise clinical precision and controlled environments, whereas others emphasise ecological validity and scalability by relying on mobile or telephonic recordings. The trade-offs involved are highlighted, and critical gaps in linguistic diversity, longitudinal follow-up, and multimodal integration are identified.

By mapping the current landscape of accessible PD speech datasets, this work supports reproducibility, benchmarking, and informed dataset selection for future studies. It also provides concrete recommendations for the development of new corpora aligned with open science practices and clinical applicability.

Keywords: Parkinson's Disease · Speech analysis · Open dataset · Voice biomarkers

1 Introduction

Parkinson's Disease (PD) impairs both motor and non-motor functions, affecting the speech production process, which worsens over time [7].

J. I. Godino Llorente (Ed.): AAPS 2024, CCIS 2646, pp. 31–50, 2026.
https://doi.org/10.1007/978-3-032-07083-8_3

Given its progressive nature, and the availability of modern signal processing and Artifical Intelligence (AI) tools, speech (comprising both voice and articulatory features) has emerged as a promising biomarker: it is non-invasive, low-cost, and easily recordable via mobile devices, making it well-suited for remote and scalable monitoring [23,36].

Numerous speech datasets have been developed to support computational approaches for screening and tracking PD. These range from high-quality recordings in controlled clinical environments to voice samples remotely collected via smartphones or telephony. However, these datasets differ substantially in accessibility, clinical detail, and linguistic scope [23,36].

Recent reviews have highlighted the frequent use of certain datasets. For instance, the 2025 review [36] found that 34% of 106 studies used data from the UC Irvine Machine Learning Repository (UCI-MLR), especially the Speech Dataset with Multiple Types of Sound Recordings, the Oxford PD Detection Dataset, and the PD Classification dataset. PC-GITA and MDVR-KCL were also widely used, appearing in 22% and 7% of the studies, respectively. Other reviews [1,4,17] have further compared model performance across voice and other data modalities.

Despite this growing literature, no study has yet offered a unified overview focused exclusively on the characteristics of publicly available PD speech datasets. Key aspects such as hosting platforms, recording protocols, task types, clinical labels, licensing terms, and language diversity remain poorly documented, hindering reproducibility and dataset selection.

This work addresses this gap by presenting a structured review of all known open-access speech datasets developed for the evaluation of PD, including PC-GITA [27], NeuroVoz [24], the Italian Database Corpus [8], the German Dataset Corpus [37], CzechPD [33], the French Dataset Corpus [16], MDVR-KCL [15], mPower [6], EWA-DB [32], and Iyer2023 [14], among others.

This work evaluates each corpus according to five dimensions: (1) demographics and dataset size; (2) recording setup and acoustic quality; (3) speech tasks and linguistic content; (4) accessibility and licensing; and (5) availability of raw audio and/or acoustic features. These criteria reflect both methodological variation and practical challenges in voice-based PD research.

The structure of this paper is as follows: Sect. 2 introduces the speech impairments in PD and the role of open datasets. Section 3 defines inclusion and exclusion criteria used to identify the corpora. Section 4 provides individual dataset descriptions. Section 5 offers a comparative analysis. And the final section discusses key aspects and future directions.

2 Background

2.1 Parkinson's Disease and Speech

PD is a progressive neurodegenerative disorder marked by the degeneration of dopaminergic neurons in the substantia nigra pars compacta, disrupting basal ganglia circuits responsible for voluntary motor control. Core motor symptoms include tremor, rigidity, and bradykinesia, but speech impairments, often appearing early, are particularly prevalent [7].

These speech impairments are categorised as hypokinetic dysarthria, a motor speech disorder commonly associated with PD and other conditions affecting the basal ganglia circuitry, although it may also result from broader dysfunctions within the extrapyramidal motor system. It affects the phonatory, articulatory, prosodic, and respiratory subsystems, leading to a flat, monotone voice, diminished vocal intensity, and breathiness or hoarseness owing to incomplete vocal folds closure and glottal irregularities [2,9,31,42].

PD disrupts the three organ systems involved in speech: the respiratory system (airflow generation), the phonatory system (vocal fold vibration), and the articulatory system (resonance and shaping by oral structures). Weakness in the larynx, soft palate, tongue, and facial muscles, often tied to damage in the striatum or globus pallidus, leads to complex speech deficits [21,23].

Articulatory impairments include slurred pronunciation and difficulty with plosives/fricatives. Speech rhythm also becomes irregular with bursts of fast speech, increased pauses, paraphasias and palilalia [5,22,38], reducing intelligibility and quality of life.

Voice changes affect 70–90% of PD patients, especially in phonation (e.g., jitter, shimmer, fundamental frequency (F0) instability), articulation (e.g., formant shifts) and prosody (e.g., monotonicity). Objective acoustic metrics such as harmonics-to-noise ratio (HNR), pathology vibrato index (PVI) and pitch period entropy (PPE) have been widely studied to quantify these symptoms [20,23,39].

In recent years, speech analysis in PD has gained prominence for both diagnosis and monitoring. Studies increasingly focus on phonation, articulation, and prosody (separately or combined) to improve detection accuracy [23]. Voice is now recognised not only as a clinical symptom, but also as a digital biomarker: objective, repeatable, non-invasive, and suitable for remote assessments.

This has fostered a surge in machine learning research for automatic detection and tracking of PD-related speech alterations, a trend accelerated by the availability of open-access voice and speech datasets across languages and conditions [11,26,34].

2.2 The Relevance of Open Datasets

Open-access speech datasets are essential for advancing computational approaches to PD detection and monitoring. Their availability ensures scientific reproducibility, enables fair algorithm benchmarking and fosters collaboration across the research community.

By providing shared resources, open datasets allow researchers to replicate experiments, verify results and identify methodological limitations under consistent conditions [30,41]. They also support standardised benchmarking, enabling fair comparisons between models and the establishment of reference baselines [3,43].

In other application domains, well-known corpora like LibriSpeech, Common Voice, TED-LIUM and VoxPopuli have enabled the training of robust, multilingual automatic speech recognition (ASR) models such as Whisper and Wav2Vec2.0 [3,30], demonstrating the transformative power of large public datasets.

In the PD domain, open datasets promote consistency in experimental design, task selection (e.g., binary classification, severity regression) and reporting practices. They also accelerate clinical translation by supporting tool validation, enabling deployment in resource-limited settings and encouraging the development of culturally and linguistically inclusive models.

Ultimately, open datasets contribute to a more transparent, equitable, and impactful application of AI in the diagnosis and monitoring of PD.

3 Dataset Selection Criteria

3.1 Search Strategy and Dataset Screening

To ensure consistency, quality and relevance across the surveyed corpora, a structured dataset selection protocol inspired by PRISMA-style systematic reviews was implemented [28]. Only corpora published between January 2010 and June 2025 were considered, focusing on datasets containing real speech recordings from individuals diagnosed with PD, optionally including Healthy Control (HC) or clinical comparison groups.

A structured Boolean search strategy was applied using the following expression:

```
("Parkinson" OR "Parkinson's Disease" OR parkinsonism) AND
("speech" OR "voice" OR "phonation" OR "spoken language") AND
("dataset" OR "database" OR "corpus" OR "recordings") AND
("open access" OR "publicly available" OR "raw audio" OR
"acoustic features") AND ("patients" OR "Healthy Control" OR
"clinical")
```

This query was adapted to the syntax and capabilities of each platform. Searches were carried out across major databases including *PubMed*, *Scopus*, *IEEE Xplore* and *arXiv*, using appropriate filters such as: publication years from 2010 onward, English language, open-access articles and clinical study types. Complementary searches were also conducted on repositories such as *Zenodo*, *PhysioNet*, *ELRA Catalogue*, *UCI-MLR*, *HuggingFace Datasets*, *Kaggle* and *GitHub*.

3.2 Inclusion and Exclusion Criteria

Only datasets that were openly accessible, either via direct download or with minimal requesting procedures, and with an academic licence were included. Datasets behind paywalls or under opaque or restrictive licences were excluded.

All included corpora contained speech recordings from individuals with confirmed PD and a matched HC group, with clear diagnostic labelling. Basic participant metadata (at least age and sex) was required, along with medication status or disease duration when available. Datasets lacking key clinical descriptors or offering only metadata (without audio or acoustic features) were excluded.

Although raw audio was preferred, datasets presenting only pre-extracted features were accepted if openly accessible, properly labelled, and based on relevant speech tasks. Priority was given to corpora including sustained phonation, diadochokinesis (DDK), reading, or spontaneous speech, provided that recording conditions and hardware specifications were documented.

3.3 Results of the Dataset Search

In total, the search yielded 180 candidate items, including datasets, articles, and repositories mentioning PD-related speech data. After deduplication and title/abstract screening, all databases not complying with the inclusion criteria described in Subsect. 3.2 were excluded.

Following full-text review and inspection of data availability, 19 datasets were retained for inclusion. These corpora span a wide linguistic range: English, Castilian Spanish, Colombian Spanish, Slovak, German, French, Italian, Mandarin Chinese, etc., and present diverse speech elicitation protocols (e.g., sustained phonation, DDK, reading aloud, naming, tongue twisters, picture description, spontaneous speech). They also vary in collection settings (clinical, home-based, telephone, mobile apps) and recording quality (studio-grade vs. ecologically valid recordings).

The filtering process and inclusion pipeline are summarised in Fig. 1.

4 Overview of PD Voice and Speech Datasets

Altogether, the dataset collection supports comprehensive analysis of PD-related speech and voice alterations. It offers a reliable testbed for the development and validation of machine learning models for detection, monitoring, and severity assessment. This section presents a summary of the key characteristics of each dataset, including speech tasks, recording setups, participant profiles, and availability. An overview of these characteristics is presented in Table 1.

4.1 Mobile Device Voice Recordings at King's College London (MDVR-KCL) [15]

The MDVR-KCL dataset, published in 2019, comprises mobile voice recordings from individuals with PD and HC collected at King's College Hospital, London.

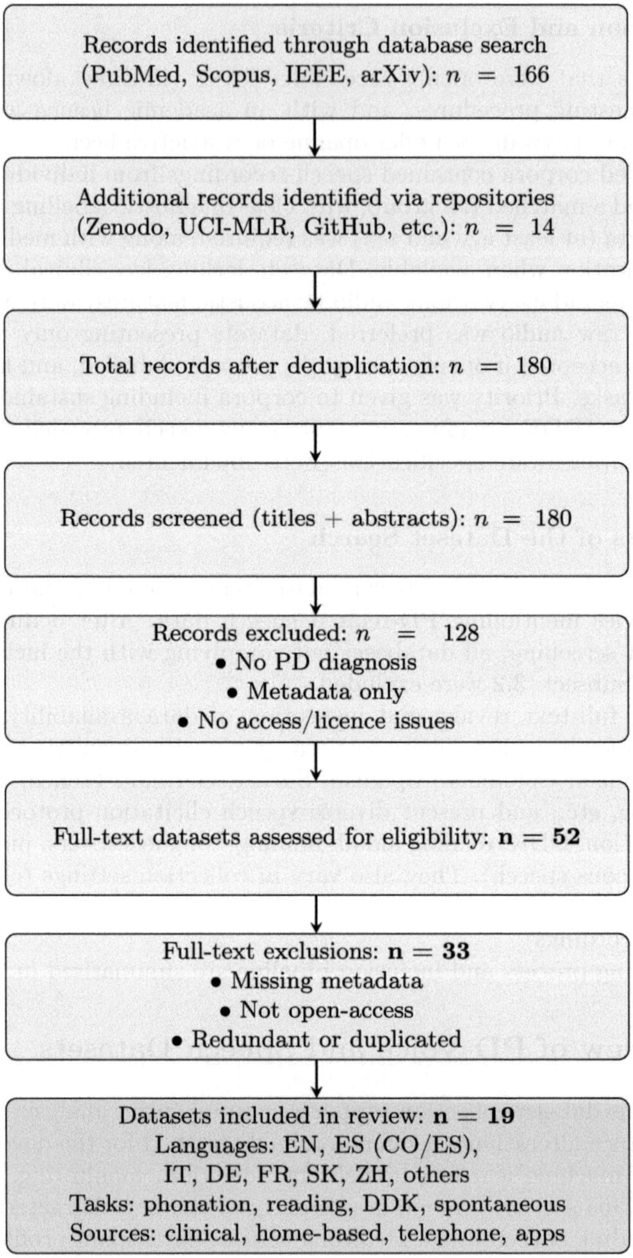

Fig. 1. Dataset selection flowchart following a PRISMA-inspired protocol.

Recordings took place in 2017 under realistic phone call conditions: participants held a smartphone to their preferred ear in a $10\,\mathrm{m}^2$ examination room with

500 ms reverberation time, ensuring consistent, close-mic placement within the reverberation radius.

Audio was captured via a Motorola Moto G4® running the 'Toggle Recording App', a custom Android® background service. Uncompressed 44.1 kHz, 16-bit WAV files were stored directly on the device's SD card, preserving raw microphone input without GSM compression.

Participants performed a standardised voice protocol during a call with a test administrator: (1) reading the passage 'The North Wind and the Sun'; (2) optionally reading a technical excerpt; and (3) engaging in a brief spontaneous dialogue. The session concluded with a farewell that triggered automatic call termination.

Clinical metadata, including subject ID, health status, Hoehn & Yahr (HY) stage and Unified Parkinson's Disease Rating Scale (UPDRS) II (item 5) and III (item 18) scores are encoded in filenames. All participants were clinically evaluated, allowing analyses beyond binary labels, as some HC presented non-zero scores and some PD scored zero on specific items.

The MDVR-KCL dataset is openly accessible[1] and offers raw audio and fine-grained clinical scores, enabling detailed machine learning analyses.

4.2 mPower Voice Data (Apple's ResearchKit®) [6]

The mPower dataset, published in 2016, is part of a large-scale, app-based longitudinal study designed to monitor PD symptoms via smartphone sensors. Developed by Sage Bionetworks using Apple's ResearchKit framework, the iOS® app enabled self-enrollment, informed consent, and unsupervised data collection. While the full study includes tapping, walking, and memory tasks, this section focuses on the voice module.

Out of 9,520 enrolled users, 6,805 completed the initial survey; 1,087 self-reported a PD diagnosis, 5,581 reported no diagnosis, and 137 declined to answer. Despite variability in adherence, 898 participants submitted data on at least five separate days within the first six months, enabling repeated, real-world sampling.

The voice task involved two steps: (1) five seconds of ambient noise recording for quality check, followed by (2) a 10-second sustained /a/ vocalization. Recordings were captured using iPhones and stored as compressed MP4 files. Each sample includes metadata such as participant ID (healthCode), timestamp, device model, app version, and medication timing (medTimepoint).

Participants with PD were instructed to perform the task three times daily (before medication, at peak effect, and randomly), with HC encouraged to follow the same schedule. This setup allows for intra-day analysis of medication effects on voice. Clinical evaluations (e.g. UPDRS, HY) are not included.

The full dataset is publicly accessible via Synapse[2].

[1] https://zenodo.org/records/2867216.
[2] https://doi.org/10.7303/syn4993293.

4.3 Italian Database Corpus [8]

Published in 2017, the Italian Database Corpus was developed to assess speech intelligibility in individuals with PD using a structured speech protocol and the Google® Speech-to-Text ASR engine. Recordings were made in quiet, echo-free environments using a custom software tool (Voxtester) that captured raw WAV audio and extracted acoustic features.

The speech protocol included: (1) two readings of a phonetically balanced Italian text; (2) DDK tasks ('pa', 'ta'); (3) sustained vowel phonation (/a/, /e/, /i/, /o/, /u/), Each vowel was produced twice: once sustained for maximum phonation time (MPT) and once constrained to 5 s; and, (4) reading of isolated words and phrases. Tasks were separated by timed pauses and designed in collaboration with clinicians and linguists.

The dataset comprises 65 participants: 28 PD patients (ages 40–80, mostly HY < 4), 22 elderly HC (60–77) and 15 young controls (19–29), all from the Puglia region. PD subjects completed the full protocol; control groups performed subsets.

Voxtester extracted features such as F1–F4, voice spectrum, DDK rate, speech duration, and vowel articulation metrics (FCR, tVSA, qVSA, VAI). Intelligibility was evaluated via ASR word error rates, revealing that slower PD speech sometimes yielded higher transcription accuracy.

The corpus includes raw WAV files and metadata (age, sex, UPDRS, speech duration) and is publicly available on IEEE Dataport[3].

4.4 CzechPD: Czech Parkinsonian Speech Dataset [33]

The CzechPD dataset (2013) was originally compiled at the General University Hospital in Prague to investigate speech alterations in individuals with idiopathic PD. Subsequent updates to the dataset expanded it to include a total of 100 participants (50 PD, 50 HC), as reported by [13]. Disease severity was assessed using the HY scale and the UPDRS-III.

Recordings were performed in a quiet clinical environment using an external condenser microphone (integrated with a Panasonic NV-GS 180® video camera) positioned approximately 15 cm from the participant's mouth. Audio was digitised at 48 kHz/16-bit resolution. Participants completed four speaking tasks: sustained phonation of vowels /a/, /i/, and /u/; DDK tasks; reading of a standardised 80-word passage; and a spontaneous monologue. Vowels were extracted following strict criteria to ensure acoustic stability.

The dataset includes high-quality raw audio recordings. Although it is not publicly available, access may be requested from the authors for non-commercial research purposes with appropriate ethical approval.

[3] https://dx.doi.org/10.21227/aw6b-tg17.

4.5 EWA-DB: Slovak Database of Speech Affected by Neurodegenerative Diseases [32]

Published in 2021, EWA-DB is a Slovak-language speech corpus developed to support research on neurodegenerative conditions, including PD, Alzheimer's disease (AD) and mild cognitive impairment (MCI). It is freely available via the ELRA repository[4].

The dataset includes 1,649 participants: 175 with PD, 87 with AD, 62 with MCI, 2 with mixed diagnosis and 1,323 HC. Demographic and clinical metadata are provided, including age, sex, education, Montreal Cognitive Assessment (MoCA) scores and self-reported speech/hearing issues.

Recordings were collected using Android®/iOS smartphones under standardised conditions (mono, 16 kHz, 16-bit Pulse Code Modulation (PCM) WAV). Participants completed 12 structured speech tasks via a mobile app, targeting motor control, cognition, and prosody. Tasks included sustained /a/ phonation, DDK (/pa-ta-ka/), counting, object/action naming, picture description, reading, and basic questions and answers.

Each task was designed to probe specific domains such as phonation stability, articulation, fluency, lexical retrieval, and discourse. Longitudinal data enable multi-session tracking for disease progression or treatment response. The corpus includes both raw audio and JSON-formatted metadata.

4.6 ICEBERG French Speech Corpus [16]

Published in 2021, the ICEBERG corpus is a French-language speech database aimed at early PD detection via acoustic biomarkers. It includes recordings from 221 native speakers: 121 with PD (diagnosed within 4 years) and 100 HC.

Two recording conditions were employed: (1) high-quality microphone recordings from 206 participants (115 PD, 91 HC) captured at 96 kHz/24-bit using a Beyerdynamics Opus 55 microphone and a Focusrite Scarlett 2i2® interface; and, (2) telephonic recordings from 162 participants (101 PD, 61 HC) collected monthly via SIP-based IVR calls made from participants' mobile phones, downsampled to 8 kHz PCM. As many participants contributed to both conditions, the total number across conditions (206 + 162) exceeds the number of 221 unique individuals in the dataset.

Speech tasks included reading, sentence repetition, free speech, and DDK tasks. The in-person protocol was more extensive, whilst the telephonic version used simplified prompts. Participants completed between 1 and 13 phone sessions (avg. 5).

Detailed metadata (age, sex, disease duration, HY, MDS-UPDRS III (OFF state) and Levodopa Equivalent Dose) is provided. Although the dataset is not publicly available, access may be requested from the authors for research purposes.

[4] https://catalogue.elra.info/en-us/repository/browse/ELRA-S0489/.

4.7 German Dataset on Prosody and Intonation in PD [37]

Published in 2011, this German-language dataset was designed to assess prosodic impairments in PD through standardised reading tasks. It includes 138 PD patients (78 males, 60 females) and 50 HC, all evaluated with the UPDRS-III and HY scale. PD participants were recorded in the ON-medication state, 60–90 min after their dopaminergic dose.

Recordings were made in quiet settings using a Plantronics Audio 550 DSP® headset and Steinberg WaveLab® software (44.1 kHz). Each participant read four syntactically complex sentences and completed two trials of MPT on vowel /a/. A subset of 20 patients underwent a levodopa challenge to assess medication effects on prosody.

Acoustic analysis was performed using PRAAT® software, with annotations including measures such as standard deviation of the F0 (F0SD) and net speech rate.

The dataset includes raw recordings and detailed acoustic measures, but is not publicly available. Access must be requested from the authors for research purposes.

4.8 Voice Samples for Patients with PD and HC. Telephonic Sustained Vowel Dataset (Iyer2023) [14]

Published in 2023, this dataset provides sustained vowel /a/ recordings captured via telephone calls from 40 individuals with PD and 41 HC. Participants left voicemails sustaining the vowel for about three seconds. Audio was sampled at 8 kHz, 16-bit, resulting in low-fidelity recordings suitable for modelling under realistic conditions.

Recordings underwent preprocessing involving noise reduction, amplitude normalization, and silence trimming. Files under 1.5 s post-trimming were excluded. The final dataset includes raw audio and 23 pre-extracted acoustic features per sample, enabling both traditional and deep learning analyses.

The corpus is publicly available via Figshare[5].

4.9 PC-GITA Corpus [27]

Published in 2014, the PC-GITA corpus is a Spanish-language speech database comprising recordings from 100 native Colombian speakers: 50 with PD and 50 HC, balanced by age and gender. Participants were clinically evaluated using the UPDRS and HY scales, with PD patients recorded in the ON-medication state.

Recordings were conducted in a soundproof booth using a Shure SM63L® microphone and an M-Audio C400® interface. Audio was saved in 44.1 kHz, 16-bit WAV format. The speech protocol covered three domains: phonation (sustained vowels with constant and variable pitch), articulation (DDK sequences, rapid syllable repetition, word reading) and prosody (sentence repetition, expressive reading, and spontaneous monologue).

[5] https://doi.org/10.6084/m9.figshare.23849127.

The corpus includes raw audio and metadata (age, gender, UPDRS-III, medication status), with each file annotated by task. Though not publicly downloadable, access is granted upon request for academic use.

4.10 NeuroVoz [24]

Published in 2024, the NeuroVoz corpus is a fully public Spanish-language speech dataset comprising recordings from 112 Castilian Spanish speakers: 54 with PD and 58 HC, matched by age and gender. All recordings were performed in the ON-medication state following dopaminergic treatment.

The protocol included four tasks: (1) sustained vowels (/a/, /e/, /i/, /o/, /u/); (2) DDK /pa-ta-ka/; (3) Listen and Repeat (LR) 16 phonetically rich phrases; and (4) spontaneous speech via picture description. Recordings were made during clinical visits using an AKG C420® headset and SoundBlaster Live® sound card at 44.1 kHz, 16-bit, yielding high-quality audio (average signal-to-noise ratio (SNR): 24.3 dB).

Metadata includes UPDRS, HY, Grade, Roughness, Breathiness, Asthenia, Strain (GRBAS), transcriptions, binary symptom labels (e.g., vocal tremor, hypophonia) and 17 voice features extracted from vowels using the AVCA-ByO toolbox [10]. The dataset contains 2,977 WAV files and is organised into raw audio, perceptual ratings, features, transcriptions (LR) and metadata.

NeuroVoz is available under FAIR principles and can be accessed via Zenodo[6].

4.11 Summary of Dataset Characteristics

The selected datasets cover a broad range of speech tasks and recording conditions. Sustained vowel phonation is common to all corpora and serves as the basis for acoustic analysis. Many also include syllable repetitions, reading, and spontaneous speech, enabling cross-task comparisons related to motor and cognitive function.

Recording setups vary from high-fidelity lab environments (e.g., CzechPD, Neurovoz, PC-GITA) to naturalistic smartphone-based settings (e.g., MDVR-KCL, mPower, EWA-DB). While the latter introduces variability, they offer better scalability and ecological validity. Sampling rates range from 16 to 48 kHz, with most data stored as uncompressed WAV files.

4.12 Other Datasets

In addition to the major open-access corpora analysed in this study, several other datasets may be of interest to the research community despite offering only pre-extracted features, lacking raw data, or being subject to restricted or conditional access.

[6] https://zenodo.org/records/10777657.

Table 1. Summary of the publicly described PD open speech datasets.

Dataset	Subjects	Language	Data type	Type of data
MDVR-KCL [15]	42 HC + 31 PD	English	Raw audio	Read passage and spontaneous dialogue; HY stage, UPDRS II/III scores
mPower [6]	5581 HC + 1087 PD	English	Raw audio	Sustained /a/ before/after medication and at arbitrary times; metadata includes timestamps and phone model
Italian Database Corpus [8]	37 HC + 28 PD	Italian	Raw audio	Sustained vowels, syllable repetition, reading tasks; intelligibility via Google ASR; acoustic metrics like tVSA, qVSA
CzechPD [33]	50 PD + 50 HC	Czech	Raw audio	Sustained phonation of vowels /a/, /i/, and /u/; DDK; reading of a standardised 80-word passage; and a spontaneous monologue
EWA-DB [32]	1323 HC + 175 PD	Slovak	Raw audio	12 diverse tasks: phonation, DDK, reading, naming, picture description; rich metadata including MoCA
ICEBERG [16]	100 HC + 121 PD	French	Raw audio	High-fidelity and telephone speech; reading, repetition, free speech, DDK tasks; UPDRS, HY, LEDD
German Prosody Dataset [37]	50 HC + 138 PD	German	Raw audio	Structured sentence reading and MPT; F0SD and net speech rate under medication
Iyer2023 [14]	41 HC + 40 PD	English	Raw audio	Sustained /a/ via voicemail (3 s); preprocessed and trimmed; 23 acoustic features extracted
PC-GITA [27]	50 HC + 50 PD	Spanish (CO)	Raw audio	Vowels, DDK (/pa-ta-ka/), isolated words, sentence repetition, spontaneous monologue
NeuroVoz [24]	58 HC + 54 PD	Spanish (ES)	Raw audio	Vowels, DDK, LR phrases, spontaneous monologue; GRBAS ratings and metadata

Mandarin Language Corpus - Tongji Hospital [44]**.** Developed at Tongji Hospital, this Mandarin-language corpus has been cited in recent studies but is not available through public repositories. It includes speech data from individuals with PD, intended for early detection research. Access may be granted upon direct request to the authors.

Korean and Taiwanese Corpus [18]**.** This bilingual dataset comprises Korean and Taiwanese speakers and was developed by specialists in neurology, speech sciences, and machine learning. Speech stimuli were language-specific and designed to capture phonetic traits relevant to PD. Although not publicly hosted, access may be requested for academic use.

InhaPD Dataset (Korea) [25]**.** The InhaPD dataset includes voice recordings from 143 Korean PD patients, categorised by HY stages 1–3 and recorded in clinical settings at 48 kHz, 32-bit resolution. Tasks included sustained vowel phonation (/a/, /i/, /u/) and reading of up to 750 Korean sentences. A total of 43 acoustic features were extracted using Parselmouth and MATLAB. Although not publicly available, the dataset may be requested from the authors under ethical research conditions.

BenSParX Dataset [12]**.** The BenSParX dataset contains 120 mono-channel recordings from 60 PD patients and 60 HC, collected in Bangladesh with Institutional Review Board (IRB) approval and informed consent. PD participants (aged 43–65) were clinically diagnosed within 1.5 years; HC (aged 41–57) had no history of neurological disease. Recordings were made via phone interviews using an Oppo F17® smartphone. Each session included responses to four open-ended health-related questions, yielding 1–2 min of spontaneous speech per answer. Audio was captured as raw 44.1 kHz, 16-bit WAV files without compression or post-processing. The dataset is publicly available via GitHub[7]. This dataset only has extracted features; however, the release of the raw data could also be suggested.

UCI-MLR Parkinson's Data Set. Five datasets hosted by the UCI-MLR fall under this category. They include features such as jitter, shimmer, HNR and Mel-Frequency Cepstral Coefficients (MFCCs), extracted from sustained phonation or other voice tasks. Although widely used in the literature, these datasets lack raw audio files, constraining signal-level modelling. A summary of their characteristics is presented in Table 2.

[7] https://github.com/Riad071/BenSParX.

Table 2. Summary of UCI-MLR Parkinson's voice datasets.

Dataset	Source, Year	Subjects	Demographics
Parkinson Dataset with Replicated Acoustic Features [29]	UCI-MLR, 2016	80 (40 PD, 40 HC)	No demographic data
Parkinson's Speech with Multiple Types of Sound Recordings [34]	UCI-MLR, 2013	Train: 20 PD / 20 HC, Test: 28 PD	Train – PD: 64.86 ± 8.97 y (43–77), 0–6 y diag.; HC: 62.55 ± 10.79 y (45–83). Test – PD: 62.67 ± 10.96 y (39–79), 0–13 y diag.
PD Classification [35]	UCI-MLR, 2018	188 PD / 64 HC	PD: 65.1 ± 10.9 y, 107 M / 81 F; HC: 61.1 ± 8.9 y, 23 M / 41 F
Oxford PD Detection Dataset [19]	UCI-MLR, 2007	31 (23 PD, 8 HC), 195 phonations	Mean age: 65.8 ± 9.8 y (range 46–85)
Parkinson's Telemonitoring [40]	UCI-MLR, 2010	42 PD (5,875 samples)	64.4 ± 9.2 y (36–85); 28 M / 14 F; unmedicated state

(a) Overview of subject characteristics in UCI-MLR Parkinson's datasets.

Dataset	Recording	Tasks	Features
[29]	Not specified	Sustained /a/, 3 repetitions	16 acoustic features; 3 samples per subject
[34]	Trust MC-1500® mic, 96 kHz, 30 dB, 10 cm	Train: 26 samples incl. vowels (/a/, /o/, /u/), numbers, words, sentences; Test: 6 samples (/a/, /o/)	26 handcrafted features per sample; UPDRS scores; no raw audio
[35]	Cerrahpaşa Univ., 44.1 kHz; recordings after neurological exam	Sustained /a/, 3 repetitions	16 features (jitter, shimmer, pitch, MFCCs); no raw audio
[19]	AKG C420® mic, 8 cm, 44.1 kHz, IAC booth; calibrated with B&K 2238	Sustained /a/, avg. 6 phonations (1–36s)	22 features (jitter, shimmer, RPDE, DFA, PPE); amplitude normalised
[40]	Intel AHTD® system, 5 cm headset mic, 24 kHz, 16-bit, at-home, weekly sessions	6 sustained /a/ phonations (4 normal, 2 loud); weekly over 6 months	16 features (jitter, shimmer, NHR, HNR, RPDE, DFA, PPE); no raw audio

(a) Technical details of UCI-MLR datasets: setup, tasks and extracted features.

5 Comparative Analysis

5.1 Demographics and Size

The datasets reviewed vary considerably in terms of sample size, demographic diversity and group composition. Large-scale datasets such as mPower (9,520 participants consented; 1,087 self-declared PD cases) and EWA-DB (1,649 participants, including 175 PD) offer substantial statistical power and demographic heterogeneity. In contrast, focused corpora like CzechPD and PC-GITA (both with 50 PD) offer smaller but clinically verified cohorts, often with balanced gender and age matching. NeuroVoz and PC-GITA are notable for their careful demographic pairing of PD and HC groups in Spanish-speaking contexts. Some datasets include multiple diagnostic categories; for example, EWA-DB includes AD and MCI), which broadens their application to differential diagnosis. Ages range from young adults (19–29 in the Italian corpus) to elderly populations (up to 80+ in the Italian corpus), ensuring coverage across the progression spectrum of PD.

5.2 Recording Protocols and Quality

Recording protocols across datasets fall into two main categories: (1) controlled, high-fidelity clinical settings using professional microphones and acoustically optimised spaces; and, (2) ecologically realistic conditions using smartphones or telephonic devices that reflect real-world constraints.

The first group includes PC-GITA, NeuroVoz, Italian Database, German dataset, CzechPD and ICEBERG. These used professional-grade headsets (e.g., Shure SM63L, AKG C420, Plantronics 550 DSP, Beyerdynamic Opus 55) and captured uncompressed WAV audio at 44.1–96 kHz and 16–24-bit resolution. Recording environments ranged from soundproof booths (PC-GITA) to quiet clinical rooms (ICEBERG), with average SNR up to 24.3 dB (NeuroVoz). Protocols controlled for speaker–mic distance, ambient noise and temperature to ensure consistency.

The second group (MDVR-KCL, mPower, EWA-DB, Iyer2023 and ICEBERG-telephonic) prioritised accessibility and scalability. These datasets were collected via smartphone apps or standard phone networks, typically at 16 or 8 kHz. MDVR-KCL captured uncompressed WAV files via Motorola. mPower used iPhones with M4A compression; Iyer2023 relied on voicemail systems over telephony, producing low-fidelity but processable 8 kHz data. EWA-DB adopted standardised mobile protocols across Android/iOS platforms and ICEBERG's telephonic subset used G.711-encoded calls, downsampled to PCM at 8 kHz.

Sampling rates across corpora range from 8 to 96 kHz. Most datasets use WAV format, with mPower as the main exception, using M4A. Clinical datasets control noise through sound-treated environments and professional-grade equipment, whereas smartphone-based datasets apply post-processing (e.g., normalization, silence trimming, noise gating). These approaches reflect complementary priorities: recording precision versus ecological validity and remote deployability.

Together, these datasets enable both fine-grained acoustic modelling and large-scale, real-world deployment of vocal biomarkers in PD.

5.3 Task Types

Speech tasks vary across datasets in complexity and purpose. Sustained vowel phonation (typically /a/) is the most common, included in all corpora except the German dataset, where it appears only as MPT. This task provides a minimal yet robust probe for assessing phonatory impairment associated with PD.

DDK tasks (e.g., /pa-ta-ka/) are present in NeuroVoz, PC-GITA, EWA-DB, ICEBERG, and CzechPD. ICEBERG features an especially rich DDK protocol with varied syllabic combinations targeting articulatory agility.

Reading tasks are included in MDVR-KCL, PC-GITA, the German corpus, Italian database, and ICEBERG. These assess intelligibility, prosody, and motor control under structured conditions. ICEBERG's protocol includes phonetically balanced paragraphs, dialogues, and expressive sentences.

Spontaneous speech, elicited via open-ended questions or picture descriptions, is present in NeuroVoz, EWA-DB, CzechPD, and ICEBERG. These tasks capture natural speech features like fluency, prosody, and lexical variability.

Datasets like NeuroVoz, PC-GITA, ICEBERG and EWA-DB use multimodal protocols encompassing phonation, articulation and prosody. In contrast, mPower and Iyer2023 include only sustained vowel tasks, favoring remote deployment but limiting phonetic diversity.

Task design often reflects dataset goals: the Italian corpus emphasises intelligibility via ASR alignment; the German dataset focuses on prosody and motor fatigue; and ICEBERG combines lab and telephonic recordings for both clinical precision and ecological validity.

5.4 Accessibility and Licensing

All datasets are publicly available, though access procedures differ. Fully open corpora include NeuroVoz and MDVR-KCL (Zenodo), mPower (Synapse), EWA-DB (ELRA), Italian Corpus (IEEE Dataport) and Iyer2023 (Figshare). Semi-open corpora include PC-GITA, CzechPD, ICEBERG, and the German corpus, all of which require a request to the developers. Licensing terms are often research-only. Some datasets (most notably NeuroVoz) are explicitly aligned with the FAIR principles, although all of them comply with FAIR to some degree. Public access enhances reproducibility and benchmarking, yet datasets like PC-GITA and CzechPD, though valuable, limit immediate accessibility. The inclusion of metadata and documentation varies, with NeuroVoz, EWA-DB, and mPower standing out for their structured organisation.

5.5 Feature Availability

A majority of datasets offer raw audio, enabling custom preprocessing and feature extraction. Exceptions include BenSParX and UCI-MLR datasets, which only offer pre-extracted features. Datasets like NeuroVoz and PC-GITA offer both raw recordings and handcrafted acoustic features (e.g., jitter, shimmer, HNR, cepstral peak prominence (CPP)). Iyer2023 includes 23 features extracted post-cleaning, whilst EWA-DB and mPower support signal reprocessing via raw waveform availability. Feature types vary from spectral and cepstral parameters to intelligibility scores (Italian corpus) and prosodic variability metrics (German corpus). The diversity of available features, combined with the presence of raw audio, enables both traditional statistical analysis and modern deep learning approaches.

6 Discussion

The reviewed datasets provide a strong foundation for developing vocal biomarkers of PD. Many offer raw audio, enabling signal-level analysis and custom feature extraction. High-fidelity corpora such as PC-GITA, NeuroVoz and CzechPD are suited for precise acoustic modelling, whilst others like mPower and Iyer2023 capture speech in ecologically valid mobile or telephonic settings, supporting real-world deployment.

Several datasets also include rich metadata (e.g., clinical scores, demographics, and perceptual ratings) enhancing their utility for supervised learning and symptom tracking. NeuroVoz and MDVR-KCL are notable in this regard.

However, limitations persist. Some datasets (e.g., UCI-MLR or BenSParX) lack raw audio, reducing reproducibility. Others, like PC-GITA and the German corpus, have restricted access. Self-reported diagnoses (mPower) may introduce labelling noise and heterogeneous protocols, hindering cross-dataset comparisons. Most datasets are small, except for EWA-DB and mPower.

There are also significant gaps. Linguistic and geographic diversity is limited, risking algorithmic bias. Longitudinal data are rare, with few recordings tracking disease progression or treatment response. Advanced-stage PD and comorbidities are underrepresented.

Task diversity is often narrow, with sustained phonation and DDK common, but spontaneous and cognitively loaded speech is less explored. Metadata such as medication timing or cognitive scores is inconsistently reported. Access remains uneven, with several datasets lacking clear licensing or requiring direct contact with authors. Annotation standards also vary, limiting interoperability.

To move forward, the following steps are recommended: (1) ensuring public availability under clear licences with standardised metadata and annotations; (2) increasing linguistic and regional diversity to improve generalizability; (3) collecting longitudinal and multimodal data; (4) combining scalable recording methods with clinical rigor; and (5) expanding task protocols to include spontaneous and cognitively demanding speech. These steps will strengthen the development of robust, interpretable, and clinically useful speech-based biomarkers for PD.

7 Conclusions

This review offers a detailed comparative analysis of publicly available speech datasets for PD, underscoring their methodological diversity, clinical richness, and relevance for computational modelling. The examined corpora vary widely in recording conditions (from studio-grade to telephonic), task design (sustained vowels, reading, spontaneous speech) and annotation depth (clinical scores, perceptual ratings, demographics).

Controlled-environment datasets like PC-GITA, NeuroVoz, and CzechPD offer high-quality audio and rich metadata, enabling precise acoustic analysis and supervised learning. Others, such as mPower and Iyer2023, emphasise scalability and ecological validity, offering realistic data for remote monitoring and mHealth applications.

Nonetheless, key challenges remain: inconsistent metadata, limited linguistic and geographic diversity, scarce longitudinal data, and frequent access restrictions. These factors hinder reproducibility, generalizability, and robust benchmarking.

Progress in voice-based PD biomarkers depends on the availability of open, standardised, and clinically annotated corpora. Future efforts should prioritise harmonization, inclusion of underrepresented populations, longitudinal design, and multimodal integration. Continued development of accessible, clinically grounded datasets will be critical to advancing diagnostic and monitoring tools based on speech.

Acknowledgments. This work was supported by the Ministry of Economy and Competitiveness of Spain under Grant PID2021-128469OB-I00, and by Comunidad de Madrid, Spain. This is also supported by a grant of the MISTI MIT Global Experiences. Universidad Politécnica de Madrid also supports Julián D. Arias-Londoño through a María Zambrano UP2021-035 grant funded by European Union-NextGenerationEU. Finally, the authors would like to thank the Madrid ELLIS unit (European Laboratory for Learning & Intelligent Systems) for its economic support to present this work at the 2nd Automatic Assessment of Parkinsonian Speech Workshop held in Cambridge, MA, USA.

Conflict of Interest. The authors declare no competing interests.

References

1. Abumalloh, R.A., et al.: Parkinson's disease diagnosis using deep learning: a bibliometric analysis and literature review. Ageing Res. Rev. **96**, 102285 (2024)
2. Adams, S.G., Dykstra, A.: Hypokinetic dysarthria. In: McNeil, M.R. (ed.) Clinical Management of Sensorimotor Speech Disorders, pp. 188–198. Thieme (2008)
3. Baevski, A., Zhou, Y., Mohamed, A., Auli, M.: wav2vec 2.0: a framework for self-supervised learning of speech representations. In: Advances in Neural Information Processing Systems, vol. 33, pp. 12449–12460 (2020)
4. Bang, C., Bogdanovic, N., Deutsch, G., et al.: Machine learning for the diagnosis of Parkinson's disease using speech analysis: a systematic review. Int. J. Speech Technol. **26**, 991–998 (2023)

5. Borsel, J.V., Bontinck, C., Coryn, M., Paemeleire, F., Vandemaele, P.: Acoustic features of palilalia: a case study. Brain Lang. **101** (2007)
6. Bot, B.M., et al.: The mpower study, Parkinson disease mobile data collected using researchkit. Sci. Data **3** (2016)
7. Darley, F.L., Aronson, A.E., Brown, J.R.: Clusters of deviant speech dimensions in the dysarthrias. J. Speech Hear. Res. **12** (1969)
8. Dimauro, G., Nicola, V.D., Bevilacqua, V., Caivano, D., Girardi, F.: Assessment of speech intelligibility in Parkinson's disease using a speech-to-text system. IEEE Access **5** (2017)
9. Duffy, J.R.: Motor Speech Disorders: Substrates, Differential Diagnosis, and Management. Elsevier, 3rd edn. (2013)
10. García, J.A.G., Moro-Velázquez, L., Arias-Londoño, J.D., Godino-Llorente, J.I.: On the design of automatic voice condition analysis systems. Part III: review of acoustic modelling strategies. Biomed. Signal Process. Control. **66**, 102049 (2021)
11. Guerrero-López, A., Arias-Londoño, J.D., Shattuck-Hufnagel, S., Godino-Llorente, J.I.: MARTA: a model for the automatic phonemic grouping of the parkinsonian speech. TechRxiv preprint (2024)
12. Hossain, R., Kabir, M.A., Mowla, A.I.G., Roy, A.C., Ghosh, R.K.: Bensparx: a robust explainable machine learning framework for Parkinson's disease detection from Bengali conversational speech (2025)
13. Ibarra, E.J., Arias-Londoño, J.D., Zañartu, M., Godino-Llorente, J.I.: Towards a corpus (and language)-independent screening of Parkinson's disease from voice and speech through domain adaptation. Bioengineering **10**(11) (2023)
14. Iyer, A., Kemp, A., Rahmatallah, Y., Prior, F., Virmani, T., Larson-Prior, L., et al.: A machine learning method to process voice samples for identification of Parkinson's disease. Sci. Rep. **13**, 20615 (2023)
15. Jaeger, H., Trivedi, D., Stadtschnitzer, M.: Mobile device voice recordings at king's college London (MDVR-KCL) from both early and advanced Parkinson's disease patients and healthy controls (2019)
16. Jeancolas, L., et al.: X-vectors: new quantitative biomarkers for early Parkinson's disease detection from speech. Front. Neuroinform. **15** (2021)
17. Kumar, R., Sharma, M., Chen, W.: Analysis of different modality of data to diagnose Parkinson's disease using machine learning and deep learning approaches: a review. Comput. Biol. Med. **158**, 107322 (2025)
18. Lim, W., Chiu, S., Peng, P., et al.: A cross-language speech model for detection of Parkinson's disease. J. Neural Transm. **132**, 579–590 (2025)
19. Little, M.: Parkinsons. UCI Machine Learning Repository (2007)
20. Little, M.A., McSharry, P.E., Hunter, E.J., Spielman, J., Ramig, L.O.: Suitability of dysphonia measurements for telemonitoring of Parkinson's disease. IEEE Trans. Biomed. Eng. **56** (2009)
21. Logemann, J., Fisher, H., Boshes, B.: The steps in the degeneration of speech and voice control in Parkinson's disease. In: Siegfried, J. (ed.) Parkinson's Disease: Rigidity, Akinesia, Behavior, pp. 63–78. Hans Huber (1973)
22. Ma, A., Lau, K.K., Thyagarajan, D.: Voice changes in Parkinson's disease: what are they telling us? (2020)
23. Majda-Zdancewicz, E., Potulska-Chromik, A., Nojszewska, M., Kostera-Pruszczyk, A.: Speech signal analysis in patients with Parkinson's disease, taking into account phonation, articulation, and prosody of speech. Appl. Sci. **14**(23), 11085 (2024)
24. Mendes-Laureano, J., et al.: Neurovoz: a castillian Spanish corpus of parkinsonian speech. Sci. Data **11** (2024)

25. Mondol, R., Kim, R., Lee, S.: Advanced optimization strategies for combining acoustic features and speech recognition error rates in multi-stage classification of Parkinson's disease severity. Biomed. Eng. Lett. **15**(2), 497–511 (2025)
26. Orozco-Arroyave, J.R., et al.: Automatic detection of Parkinson's disease in running speech spoken in three different languages. J. Acoust. Soc. Am. **139** (2016)
27. Orozco-Arroyave, J.R., Arias-Londoño, J.D., Vargas-Bonilla, J.F., González-Rátiva, M.C., Nöth, E.: New Spanish speech corpus database for the analysis of people suffering from Parkinson's disease. In: Calzolari, N., et al. (eds.) Proceedings of the Ninth International Conference on Language Resources and Evaluation (LREC 2014), pp. 342–347. European Language Resources Association (ELRA) (2014)
28. Page, M.J., et al.: The PRISMA 2020 statement: an updated guideline for reporting systematic reviews. BMJ **372** (2021)
29. Prez, C.: Parkinson Dataset with replicated acoustic features. UCI Machine Learning Repository (2016)
30. Radford, A., Kim, J.W., Xu, T., Brockman, G., McLeavey, C., Sutskever, I.: Robust speech recognition via large-scale weak supervision. In: Proceedings of the 40th International Conference on Machine Learning. ICML 2023. JMLR.org (2023)
31. Rhonda, J.H., Oates, J.M., Debbie, J.P., Andrew, J.H.: Voice characteristics in the progression of Parkinson's disease. Int. J. Lang. Commun. Disord. **35** (2000)
32. Rusko, M., et al.: Slovak database of speech affected by neurodegenerative diseases. Sci. Data **11**, 1320 (2024)
33. Rusz, J., et al.: Imprecise vowel articulation as a potential early marker of Parkinson's disease: effect of speaking task. J. Acoust. Soc. Am. **134**(3), 2171–2181 (2013)
34. Sakar, B.E., et al.: Collection and analysis of a Parkinson speech dataset with multiple types of sound recordings. IEEE J. Biomed. Health Inform. **17** (2013)
35. Sakar, C., Serbes, G., Gunduz, A., Nizam, H., Sakar, B.: Parkinson's Disease Classification. UCI Machine Learning Repository (2018)
36. Silva, A., Gómez, L., Pereira, J.: Voice analysis in Parkinson's disease: a systematic literature review. J. Biomed. Speech Process. **12**(1), 1–26 (2025)
37. Skodda, S., Grönheit, W., Schlegel, U.: Intonation and speech rate in Parkinson's disease: general and dynamic aspects and responsiveness to levodopa admission. J. Voice **25** (2011)
38. Skodda, S., Schlegel, U.: Speech rate and rhythm in Parkinson's disease. Mov. Disord. **23** (2008)
39. Tsanas, A., Little, M.A., Ramig, L.O.: Remote assessment of Parkinson's disease symptom severity using the simulated cellular mobile telephone network. IEEE Access **9** (2021)
40. Tsanas, A., Little, M.A., McSharry, P.E., Ramig, L.O.: Accurate telemonitoring of Parkinson's disease progression by noninvasive speech tests. IEEE Trans. Biomed. Eng. **57**(4), 884–893 (2010)
41. Ulasik, M.A., Hürlimann, M., Germann, F., Gedik, E., Benites, F., Cieliebak, M.: CEASR: a corpus for evaluating automatic speech recognition. In: Calzolari, N., et al. (eds.) Proceedings of the Twelfth Language Resources and Evaluation Conference, pp. 6477–6485. European Language Resources Association, Marseille, France (2020)
42. Vizza, P., et al.: Methodologies of speech analysis for neurodegenerative diseases evaluation. Int. J. Med. Inform. **122** (2019)
43. Wang, D., Zhao, Z., Yu, W., Guo, P.: Transformers in speech processing: a survey. IEEE/ACM Trans. Audio Speech Lang. Process. **30**, 2280–2310 (2022)
44. Wang, Q., et al.: Early detection of Parkinson's disease from multiple signal speech: Based on mandarin language dataset. Front. Aging Neurosci. **14** (2022)

Attention Maps for Explainable Classification of Parkinson's Disease Using Mel Filterbank-Based CTNets

A. Patiño-Bedoya(✉), A.M. Alvarez-Meza, and G. Castellanos-Dominguez

Sede Manizales Signal Processing and Recognition Group, Universidad Nacional de Colombia, Bogotá, Colombia
alpatinob@unal.edu.co

Abstract. Recent advances position speech analysis as a promising non-invasive biomarker for Parkinson's disease (PD), with deep learning (DL) models achieving notable classification performance. However, the inherent complexity of such models underscores the need for robust explainability to ensure clinical interpretability, trust, and real-world applicability. To address this limitation, we extract saliency maps from Transformer-based models to visualize key time-frequency regions, thereby identifying clinically meaningful features for PD diagnosis. Specifically, we evaluate CTNets, which integrate convolutional layers for localized spectro-temporal feature extraction with Transformer-based attention mechanisms to capture long-range dependencies. To enhance model explainability, we assess three activation mapping techniques: Layer-wise Relevance Propagation, Gradient-weighted Class Activation Mapping, and Score-weighted Class Activation Mapping. Validation across two real-world datasets reveals a high degree of consistency in attention patterns, underscoring CTNet's capacity to combine advanced ML methodologies with clinically relevant neurological assessment. By ensuring interpretability and demonstrating robust generalization across multilingual clinical datasets, the CTNet framework establishes a reliable foundation for computer-aided PD detection.

Keywords: Mel-spectrum · CTNets · Activation Maps · Parkinson Disease

1 Introduction

Recent research has increasingly focused on speech analysis as a non-invasive biomarker for Parkinson's disease (PD), supported by the growing adoption of deep learning (DL) models to enhance classification accuracy [6]. While DL architectures have proven effective in capturing subtle vocal impairments, their inherent complexity raises concerns regarding explainability, which is critical to ensure clinical interpretability, trust, and translational applicability [18].

J. I. Godino Llorente (Ed.): AAPS 2024, CCIS 2646, pp. 51–65, 2026.
https://doi.org/10.1007/978-3-032-07083-8_4

Given that Parkinson's Disease (PD) symptoms may manifest across non-contiguous regions of the spectrogram, Transformer architectures offer a distinct advantage through their self-attention mechanism, which models global spectrotemporal dependencies. This capability enables the detection of dispersed vocal anomalies—such as tremor, jitter, and spectral instability—more effectively than conventional architectures [19]. By leveraging global context modeling, Transformer-based models can capture more discriminative representations of PD-related speech impairments than traditional convolutional neural networks (CNNs), consistently outperforming them in this domain [2]. Moreover, the lightweight nature of fine-tuned, pretrained Transformers, combined with the non-invasive input modality of speech, positions these models as ideal candidates for remote screening applications. Their compatibility with standard GPUs and low-memory devices further facilitates real-time PD risk assessment in telehealth settings [17].

Nonetheless, several challenges limit the deployment of Transformer-based models in clinical practice. First, despite their parameter efficiency, fine-tuning pretrained Transformers demands substantial amounts of high-quality, labeled PD speech data. The limited availability and heterogeneity of publicly accessible corpora increase the risk of overfitting and hinder generalization to unseen speakers or recording conditions [6]. Second, the quadratic computational complexity of self-attention with respect to sequence length may introduce inference latency on standard CPUs, often necessitating GPU acceleration and thereby reducing feasibility for real-time or resource-constrained applications [10]. Moreover, the acoustic variability inherent to telehealth recordings—including differences in microphone quality, background noise, and speaking styles—can significantly degrade model performance unless mitigated through robust data augmentation or domain adaptation strategies [5]. Critically, despite the availability of attention weights, the interpretability of Transformer models remains limited. Their decision-making processes are often perceived as opaque "black boxes," potentially undermining clinical trust and necessitating complementary validation approaches, such as rule-based mechanisms or spectral-feature attribution methods [4].

To address the critical limitation of interpretability, this study leverages the extraction of saliency maps from Transformer-based models to visualize key time–frequency regions, thereby offering clinically meaningful features for PD diagnosis. Specifically, we evaluate CTNets, which combine convolutional layers for localized spectro-temporal feature detection (e.g., tremors, phonatory instability) with Transformer attention for modeling long-range dependencies (e.g., prosodic variations) [22]. In addition, we aim to enhance the clinical interpretability of CTNets by generating attention maps that visualize spatiotemporal PD biomarkers, as previously suggested in [3]. We systematically evaluate three state-of-the-art explainability methods compared in [14]—Layer-wise Relevance Propagation (LRP), Gradient-weighted Class Activation Mapping (Grad-CAM), and Score-weighted Class Activation Mapping (Score-CAM). Validation on two real-world datasets reveals a high degree of consistency in the extracted attention patterns, underscoring CTNet's ability to integrate advanced ML methodologies with practical neurological assessment. By ensuring interpretability alongside robust and generalizable performance across multilingual clinical contexts, the CTNet framework offers a trustworthy and clinically relevant foundation for computer-aided PD detection.

2 Methods

CTNet for 2D Spectro-temporal Representations

CTNet models process 2D spectro-temporal representations $\mathbf{X}\in\mathbb{R}^{T\times F}$ through a hybrid architecture combining convolutional feature extraction with transformer-based attention, according to the next pipeline [21]:

1. Hybrid Input Representation:

- Mel-Spectrogram Computation estimated as below:

$$\epsilon_m = \sum_{k=0}^{N/2} B_m[k] \cdot |X[m,k]|^2, \quad m = 1, \ldots, M$$

  where $B_m[k]$ are Mel-spaced triangular filters with $f_{\text{mel}}(f)=2595\log_{10}(1+f/700)$.
- Convolutional Stem: $\mathbf{X}'=\text{Conv2D}(\mathbf{X})\in\mathbb{R}^{T'\times F'\times d}$. This operation, specific to CTNet, employs strided convolutions to reduce the temporal and frequency dimensions while preserving the local spectro-temporal structure of the input representation.

2. Position-Aware Projection: $\mathbf{H}0 = \mathbf{X}'\mathbf{W}_p + \mathbf{E}_t + \mathbf{E}_f + \mathbf{E}\text{loc}$, where $\mathbf{E}_{\text{loc}}$ encodes local patch positions (unique to CTNet's convolutional embedding).

3. Convolution-Augmented Transformer Layers: Each Transformer layer l performs the following computations:

$$\begin{aligned}
\mathbf{H}_l^{\text{conv}} &= \text{Conv}(\mathbf{H}_{l-1}) \quad \text{(local context refinement)} \\
\mathbf{H}_l^{\text{attn}} &= \text{MultiHeadAttention}(\mathbf{H}_l^{\text{conv}}) \\
\mathbf{H}_l' &= \text{LayerNorm}(\mathbf{H}_l^{\text{attn}} + \mathbf{H}_{l-1}) \\
\mathbf{H}_l &= \text{LayerNorm}(\text{FFN}(\mathbf{H}_l') + \mathbf{H}_l')
\end{aligned}$$

where FFN denotes a position-wise feedforward network.

4. Spectro-Temporal Attention, which may include the following variants:
- Factorized Attention (CTNet): $\mathbf{A} = \mathbf{A}_t \otimes \mathbf{A}_f$ (Kronecker product of temporal and spectral attention)
- Cross-Channel Attention: $\mathbf{H}_l^{\text{channel}} = \text{Attention}(\mathbf{Q}_c, \mathbf{K}_c, \mathbf{V}_c)$

5. Hierarchical Output Head, computed by the following activation-wise operation:

$$p(y|\mathbf{X}) = \varrho\left(\text{GAP}(\mathbf{H}_L^T) + \text{GMP}(\mathbf{H}_L^F)\right)\mathbf{W}_c$$

where GAP and GMP denote global average pooling and global max pooling applied over the temporal (T) and frequency (F) dimensions, respectively. ϱ stands for the softmax activation function

Mel-filterbank-based CTNet with Attention Maps

The CTNet attention map extraction is formally defined as follows [1]:
1. *Multi-Head Attention Maps*: For each attention head $h \in \{1, \ldots, H\}$ at layer l:

$$\mathbf{A}_l^h = \varrho\left(\frac{\mathbf{Q}_l^h(\mathbf{K}_l^h)^\top}{\sqrt{d_k}}\right) \in \mathbb{R}^{T \times T}$$

where $\mathbf{Q}l^h{=}\mathbf{H}l - 1\mathbf{W}l^{Q,h}$, $\mathbf{K}_l^h{=}\mathbf{H}l - 1\mathbf{W}_l^{K,h}$ with learnable weights $\mathbf{W}_l^{Q,h}, \mathbf{W}_l^{K,h} \in \mathbb{R}^{d \times d_k}$.
2. *Factorized Spectro-Temporal Attention*:

$$\mathbf{A}_l^{\text{time}} = \varrho\left(\frac{\mathbf{E}_t\mathbf{W}_l^{Q_t}(\mathbf{E}_t\mathbf{W}_l^{K_t})^\top}{\sqrt{d_t}}\right) \in \mathbb{R}^{T \times T}, \quad \mathbf{A}_l^{\text{freq}} = \varrho\left(\frac{\mathbf{E}_f\mathbf{W}_l^{Q_f}(\mathbf{E}_f\mathbf{W}_l^{K_f})^\top}{\sqrt{d_f}}\right) \in \mathbb{R}^{F \times F}$$

which combined via Kronecker product, that is, $\mathbf{A}_l^{\text{CT}} = \mathbf{A}_l^{\text{time}} \otimes \mathbf{A}_l^{\text{freq}} \in \mathbb{R}^{(T \cdot F) \times (T \cdot F)}$
3. *Convolutional Attention Gates* computed as: $\mathbf{M}l{=}\varrho(\text{Conv}(\mathbf{H}l - 1)) \in \mathbb{R}^{T \times F \times d}$.
4. *Cross-Layer Aggregation* estimated by the average: $\bar{\mathbf{A}}{=}\mathbb{E}\{\mathbf{M}_l \odot \text{resize}(\mathbf{A}_l^{\text{CT}}) : \forall l \in L\}$, $\bar{\mathbf{A}} \in \mathbb{R}^{T \times F \times d}$ with $\odot$ being Hadamard product and resize$(\cdot)$ adjusting dimensions, and $\mathbb{E}\{\cdot\}$ is the expectation operator.
5. *Visualization Metrics* computed by the following mean estimates:

$$\begin{aligned}
\text{Temporal focus: } \tau_t &= \mathbb{E}\{\bar{\mathbf{A}}[t, f, :] : \forall f\} \\
\text{Spectral focus: } \phi_f &= \mathbb{E}\{\bar{\mathbf{A}}[t, f, :] : \forall t\} \\
\text{Head relevance: } \gamma_h &= \frac{\|\mathbf{A}L^h\|_F}{\sum h' = 1^H \|\mathbf{A}_L^{h'}\|_F}
\end{aligned}$$

6. *Performance Metrics*:

$$\text{Precision}{=}\text{TP}/(\text{TP}{+}\text{FP}), \text{Recall}{=}\text{TP}/(\text{TP}{+}\text{FN}), \ \text{F1-score}{=}2\text{PrecRec}/\text{Prec}{+}\text{Rec}$$

3 Experimental Set-Up

This work compares the classification of subjects with PD and healthy control cases using transforms in combination with various attention maps, to improve the interpretability of inference results. The methodology, depicted in Fig. 1, proceeds in three stages: (i) initial data preprocessing; (ii) iterative training of the CT-Net model, with comparative testing of the attention maps at each iteration; and (iii) final performance assessment based on the best-performing model.

Evaluated Audio Datasets

For validation, two audio databases already referenced in the state-of-the-art in PD classification are tested:

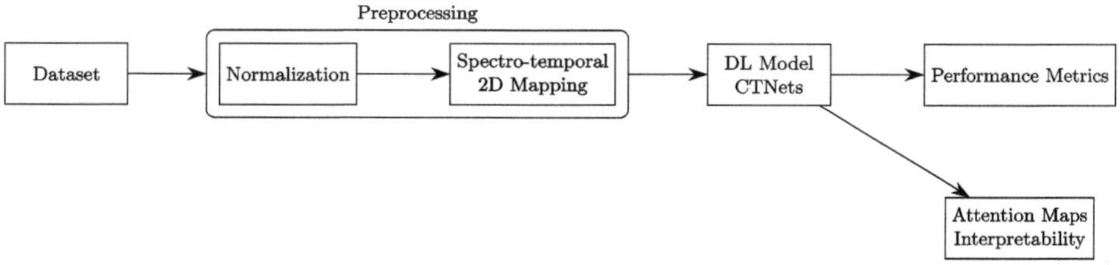

Fig. 1. Pipeline for Parkinson's disease classification using CTNets, including the performed stages for validation of attention map generation for model interpretability.

PC-GITA [13]**:** This study utilizes the PC-GITA corpus, which comprises speech recordings from 50 individuals diagnosed with PD and 50 healthy controls (HC), all native speakers of Colombian Spanish. Participants were asked to perform a series of speech tasks, including: a) Rapid repetition of syllables (/pa-ta-ka/, /pe-ta-ka/, /pa-ka-ta/, /pa/, /ta/, and /ka/), b) Reading a 36-word text, and c) Producing a spontaneous monologue. All recordings were conducted while the PD patients were in the ON medication state—that is, under the effects of their regular pharmacological treatment.

NeuroVoz [11]**:** This corpus comprises recordings from 112 native Castilian Spanish speakers (54 PD patients and 58 HC), all captured during their medication-optimized (ON) state while performing standardized speech tasks. Participants completed: (1) sustained phonation of Spanish vowels (/a/, /e/, /i/, /o/, /u/); (2) diadochokinetic tests (/pa-ta-ka/ repetitions); (3) 16 listen-and-repeat utterances (manually transcribed by clinicians); and (4) spontaneous monologues (automatically transcribed using Whisper). The corpus includes comprehensive metadata spanning demographic information (sex, age, occupation), clinical characteristics (diagnosis type, disease duration, UPDRS-III score, Hoehn and Yahr stage), symptom profiles (tremors, sialorrhea, dysphagia, hypophonia), and treatment details (medication status, vocal-fold assessments). Containing 3,010 audio recordings (26.88 ± 3.35 per participant), NeuroVoz provides a robust platform for investigating Parkinson's disease effects across multiple speech dimensions. The dataset's combination of controlled speech tasks, spontaneous speech samples, and rich clinical metadata enables comprehensive analysis of phonatory, articulatory, and prosodic features, offering valuable insights into PD-related speech impairments.

Table 1 summarizes the representative demographics and clinical scores for each tested dataset. It is worth mentioning that, in both databases, all of the patients were diagnosed by neurologist experts and were labeled according to the UPDRS and H&Y scales.

Preprocessing and Selected CTNet Model Architecture

In this study, both tested corpora underwent a rigorous preprocessing pipeline to ensure high-quality, comparable inputs for Parkinson's disease classification. All

Table 1. Demographics and clinical scores for PC-GITA and NeuroVoz datasets

	PC-GITA		NeuroVoz	
	PD	HC	PD	HC
Subjects (M)	25	25	33	28
Subjects (F)	25	25	20	26
Range of age (M)	33–81	31–86	59–86	31–86
Range of age (F)	49–75	49–76	41–88	53–77
Age (M) Mean (SD)	61.3 (11.4)	60.5 (11.6)	70.67 (7.96)	66.44 (12.32)
Age (F) Mean (SD)	60.7 (7.3)	61.4 (7.0)	71.88 (11.81)	61.6 (7.42)
Duration of disease (T) (M) Mean (SD)	8.7 (5.9)	–	6.4 (6.4)	–
Duration of disease (T) (F) Mean (SD)	12.6 (11.6)	–	6.4 (6.4)	–
MDS-UPDRS-III (M) Mean (SD)	37.8 (22.1)	–	16.9 (11.5)	–
MDS-UPDRS-III (F) Mean (SD)	37.6 (14.1)	–	16.9 (11.5)	–

recordings—originally captured at 44.1 kHz with 16-bit resolution in a soundproof booth—were manually curated to remove coughs, artifacts, and prolonged silences. Subsequently, segments of sustained vowels and other speech tasks were extracted using overlapping frames: 40 ms windows with 20 ms overlap for noise-related metrics, and 150 ms windows with 75 ms overlap for periodicity-related metrics. These segments were then downsampled to 22 kHz, amplitude-normalized (min-max), and converted into mel-spectrograms, fixing 128 of mel bands. Following recent work by [7], silences were trimmed as an initial step prior to spectrogram computation.

Though the CTNet model is not explicitly designed for audio, its hybrid CNN-Transformer structure can be suited for audio classification, considering the following steps:

- Input Audio Processing. Raw audio converted into 2-D representations, as described above, into a format suitable for convolutional layers, capturing both temporal and frequency-domain features.
- CNN-based extraction of low-level and mid-level features from the input, using 2D convolutional layers, depth-wise convolution, and pooling layers.
- Transformer encoder for capturing long-range dependencies in the high-level features, using multi-head attention, positional encoding, feed-forward networks, and layer normalization and residual connections to stabilize training and allow deeper networks by normalizing outputs and adding skip connections.
- CNN-Transformer integration module that combines the CNN's strength in local feature extraction with the Transformer's ability to capture global context.
- Output layer that consists of a fully connected layer or global average pooling to reduce the feature maps to a fixed-size vector, followed by a softmax or sigmoid layer for classification.

Table 2 summarizes the model architecture selected to ensure stable and generalizable training for audio tasks, effectively handling variability in both tested datasets.

Table 2. Optimized CTNet block diagram with consistent dimensions and selected hyperparameters.

Block	Input Size	Output Size
Input (mel-spec)	$128 \times 229 \times 1$	$128 \times 229 \times 1$
Conv Block 1	$128 \times 229 \times 1$	$42 \times 76 \times 64$
Conv Block 2	$42 \times 76 \times 64$	$14 \times 25 \times 64$
Reshape	$14 \times 25 \times 64$	350×64
Transformer Block	350×64	350×64
Flatten	350×64	22 400
Dense + Dropout	22 400	128
Final Dense (softmax)	128	2

For training purposes, the resulting feature sets were shuffled and partitioned into stratified five-fold cross-validation splits, ensuring balanced representation of both healthy and Parkinson's recordings within each fold. A Bayesian hyperparameter optimization procedure was conducted for each fold, exploring key architectural and training parameters: number of convolutional blocks (1–3), activation function (ReLU, GELU), number of attention heads (1–4), Transformer embedding dimension (64, 128), dropout rate (0.1, 0.2, 0.3), classification block units (64, 96, 128), and initial learning rate (1×10^{-3}, 4×10^{-4}, 1×10^{-4}). The best-performing configuration was then retrained and evaluated through 5-fold cross-validation.

Within each batch (batch size fixed at 32), samples were randomly shuffled. For each fold, an independent model was trained for 100 epochs using the Adam optimizer, initialized with a learning rate of 4×10^{-4}. Two training callbacks—`ReduceLROnPlateau` and `ModelCheckpoint`—were employed to dynamically adjust the learning rate and preserve the best-performing model weights. Additionally, model interpretability was enhanced using gradient-based visualization[1] and layer-wise relevance propagation (LRP)[2], with visual outputs generated using `matplotlib.pyplot`. All training experiments were conducted on the Kaggle platform using dual NVIDIA T4 GPUs, under Python 3.10, TensorFlow 2.8.3, Keras Tuner 3.8, and Keras-vis 0.8.7.

[1] Grad-CAM via `tf_keras_vis.gradcam.Gradcam`.

[2] LRP via `tf_keras_vis.saliency.Saliency`.

4 Results and Discussion

Tuning of CTNet-based Classifier

To ensure credible interpretability, the proposed Transformer-based architecture was carefully tuned to achieve performance comparable to state-of-the-art models. Table 3 presents our classification results for distinguishing HC from PD subjects using the CTNet-based approach, which are compared against several recently tested deep learning architectures validated on the PC-GITA database. The performance metrics for classification used are F1-score, recall, and Precision.

Notably, CTNet achieves the highest overall performance, with an F1-score of 0.84—surpassing the Vision Transformer baseline by six percentage points. The closely balanced precision and recall values indicate that CTNet effectively minimizes both false positives and false negatives, providing a more reliable decision boundary between PD and HC classes.

Table 3. Comparison of DL architectures in the classification PD vs. HC, validated on the PC-GITA database [8].

Architecture	*F1-Score*	*Recall*	*Precision*
EfficientNetV1	0.69	0.71	0.68
Swin Transformer	0.68	0.76	0.62
ResNet18	0.70	0.71	0.69
ResNet50	0.72	0.71	0.72
Vision Transformer	0.78	0.78	0.77
CTNet	**0.84**	**0.84**	**0.85**

Overall, the proposed classifier consistently outperforms baseline and comparative models across all evaluation metrics, reflecting not only improved classification accuracy but also enhanced robustness and generalization when applied to diverse speech patterns.

Interpretability Enhanced by Attention Maps for PC-GITA

For the PC-GITA dataset, interpretability is assessed through LRP visualizations. Figure 2a (top row) shows the point-wise averaged LRP maps for HC subjects, while Fig. 2b presents the corresponding maps for PD patients. In Fig. 2a, three salient regions emerge for HC recordings. The model consistently emphasizes a broad mid-frequency band (approximately 500–1000 Hz) across central time frames (60–140), reflecting stable formant trajectories and harmonic structures characteristic of healthy phonation. These acoustic patterns are likely leveraged by CTNet as robust indicators of unimpaired speech. A secondary band of relevance is observed in the upper mid-frequency range (1800–2100 Hz) during frames 120–240, suggesting sensitivity to high-order harmonics and spectral tilt—features commonly associated with vocal clarity. Conversely, the onset (frames 0–20) and offset (frames 200–220) segments exhibit minimal relevance, consistent with the absence of pathological glottal anomalies in HC speech.

Figure 2b reveals a markedly different saliency distribution for PD subjects. LRP maps highlight the low-frequency range (below 500 Hz), especially between frames 40–100, likely reflecting irregular glottal vibrations and vocal tremor—core markers of Parkinsonian dysphonia. In addition, high relevance is assigned to both the onset (frames 0–40) and offset (frames 180–240) regions, indicating the model's sensitivity to disrupted phonatory transitions such as delayed initiation and premature termination. Unlike the HC patterns, the mid- and high-frequency bands in PD recordings show diminished and inconsistent activation, aligning with the spectral degradation and aperiodicity typically observed in pathological speech.

Together, these findings confirm that CTNet relies on physiologically and acoustically meaningful spectro-temporal regions to distinguish HC from PD speech. The LRP maps in Fig. 2 enhance the transparency of the model's decisions and support its clinical applicability by localizing salient features linked to phonatory health and impairment.

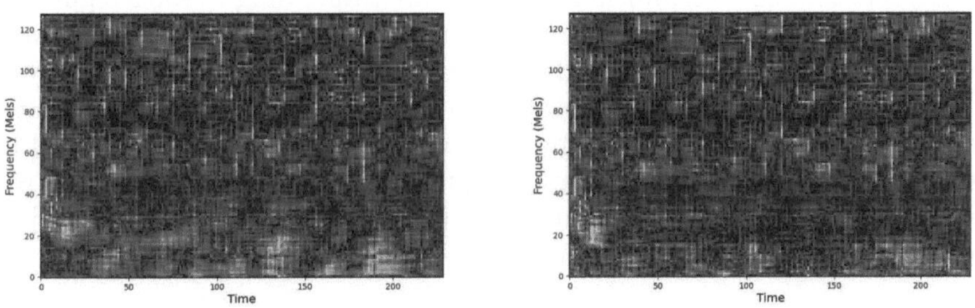

(a) HC **(b)** PD

Fig. 2. Point-wise Averaged LRP saliency maps (mel-spectrograms) for (a) HC and (b) PD recordings. Regions of high relevance correspond to frequency–time zones most influential in model decision-making.

Fig. 3 presents Grad-CAM visualizations derived from the final convolutional layer of CTNet, offering insight into the spatial attention patterns that precede the model's classification decisions. For healthy control subjects (Fig. 3a), the Grad-CAM activations exhibit concentrated, well-defined regions primarily focused on the central temporal frames and stable mid-frequency bands (approximately 500–1500 Hz). This localized activation pattern aligns with the presence of consistent formant structures and harmonic stability characteristic of normal phonation. The network's convolutional layers appear to effectively capture the regular spectro-temporal patterns associated with healthy vocal tract function,

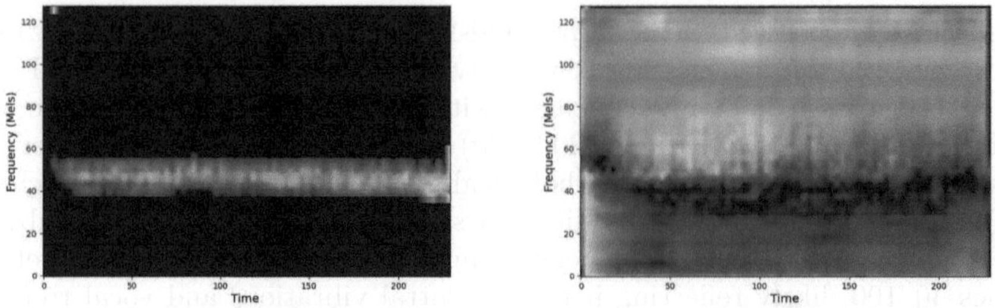

(a) HC (b) PD

Fig. 3. Grad-CAM activations from the last convolutional layer of CTNet applied to Mel-spectrograms. (a) depicts HC subjects. (b) depicts PD patients.

demonstrating focused attention on acoustically rich regions that support robust speech production.

In contrast, the Grad-CAM visualizations for PD patients (Fig. 3b) reveal a markedly different activation distribution characterized by more dispersed and fragmented attention patterns. The activations extend toward lower frequency regions (below 500 Hz) and show increased sensitivity to temporal boundaries, particularly at speech onset and offset segments. This broader spatial distribution suggests that the convolutional features are responding to the irregular glottal patterns, reduced vocal stability, and articulatory timing deficits commonly observed in Parkinsonian dysphonia. Notably, the less concentrated activation pattern reflects the network's adaptation to the increased variability and reduced predictability inherent in pathological speech signals. The aforementioned findings are consistent with those reported in previous studies [9,12,15,16,20], which similarly identified salient low-to-mid frequency characteristics in PD and mid-frequency patterns in HC populations.

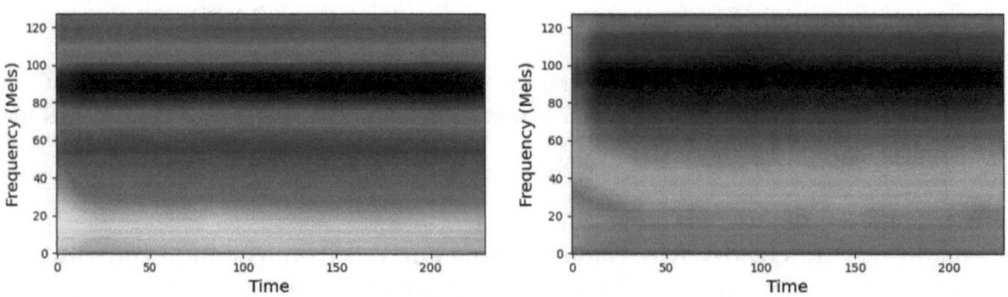

(a) HC subjects. (b) PD subjects.

Fig. 4. Score-CAM activations from the last convolutional layer of CTNet applied to Mel-spectrograms extracted from HC and PD patients.

Complementing the LRP and Grad-CAM visualizations, Fig. 4 presents Score-CAM activations, highlighting mel-spectrogram regions that most significantly influence CTNet's classification. For HC subjects (Fig. 4a), activations are localized and consistent, primarily within the mid-frequency range (500–1500 Hz; ∼20–50 mel bins) across central frames (60–160). These regions align with stable formant trajectories and harmonic structures seen in LRP (Fig. 2a) and Grad-CAM (Fig. 3a), reflecting spectral regularity in healthy speech. A secondary band appears in the higher mid-range (1800–2200 Hz; ∼60–70 mel bins, frames 120–200), indicating sensitivity to spectral tilt and high-order harmonics. Onset (0–20) and offset (200–229) segments show minimal activation, consistent with the absence of glottal or articulatory irregularities.

For PD subjects (Fig. 4b), activations are more dispersed, with emphasis on low-frequency regions (<500 Hz; ∼0–20 mel bins) during frames 40–120, corresponding to vocal tremor and glottal instability. Additional relevance at onset and offset (0–40, 180–229) reflects sensitivity to phonatory transitions. Unlike HC, mid- and high-frequency bands (500–2000 Hz; ∼20–65 mel bins) show reduced and inconsistent activation, indicating spectral degradation. This broader, less focused pattern suggests CTNet captures clinically meaningful features linked to the variability and aperiodicity of PD speech.

Interpretability Enhanced by Attention Maps for Neurovoz

Analysis of the NeuroVoz dataset using three complementary visualization techniques reveals patterns that both validate PC-GITA findings and highlight dataset-specific characteristics. The LRP maps for HC subjects (Fig. 5a) exhibit well-defined activation patterns concentrated in the mid-frequency range (500–1500 Hz) across central temporal frames (50–180), corresponding to stable formant structures characteristic of healthy Castilian Spanish phonation. The model shows particular sensitivity to spectral regions around 800–1200 Hz during frames 80–160, capturing consistent vowel formants and articulatory precision. Compared to PC-GITA, these HC subjects display slightly extended temporal activation, likely reflecting NeuroVoz's diverse speech tasks including sustained phonation and diadochokinetic sequences.

Conversely, PD subjects (Fig. 5b) reveal characteristic pathological markers through high relevance assigned to low-frequency regions (below 400 Hz) during frames 30–120, consistent with vocal tremor and irregular glottal oscillations. The model demonstrates heightened sensitivity to onset (0–50) and offset (160–220) segments, indicating impaired phonatory transitions that align with NeuroVoz's documented clinical symptoms including hypophonia and dysphagia.

Grad-CAM visualizations (Fig. 5c–d) provide complementary insights into convolutional feature extraction. HC subjects (Fig. 5c) show concentrated activations within mid-frequency bands (600–1400 Hz), capturing stable spectro-temporal patterns and consistent formant transitions across NeuroVoz's diverse speech tasks. In contrast, PD subjects (Fig. 5d) exhibit dispersed and fragmented activations extending toward lower frequencies (below 500 Hz) with increased

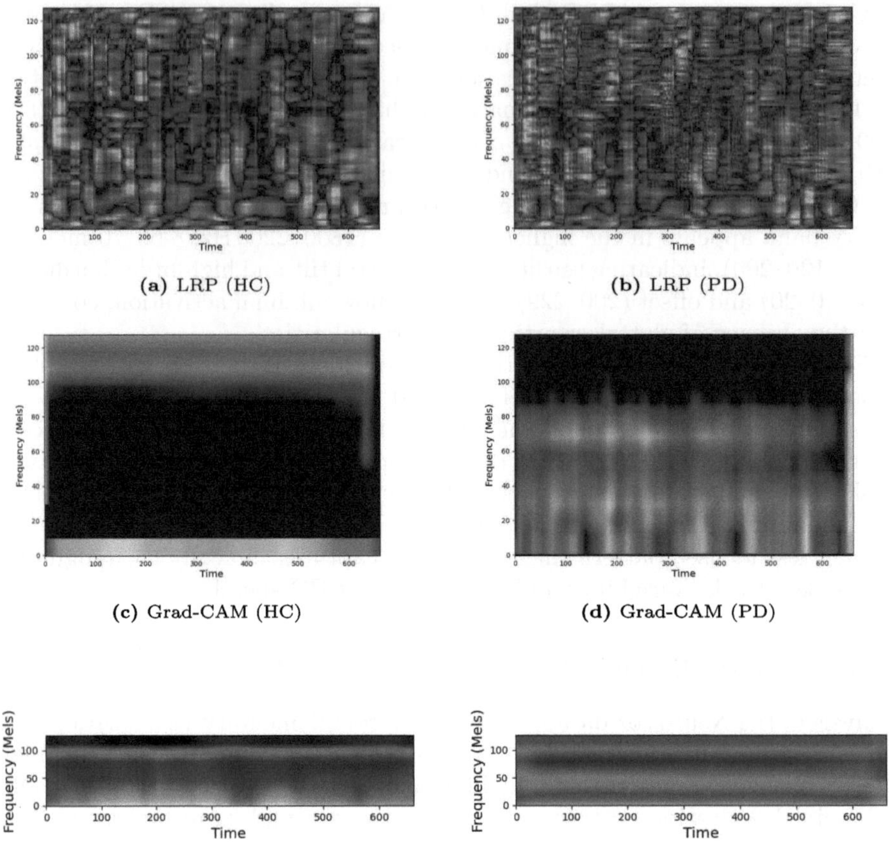

(a) LRP (HC) **(b)** LRP (PD)

(c) Grad-CAM (HC) **(d)** Grad-CAM (PD)

(e) Score-CAM (HC) **(f)** Score-CAM (PD)

Fig. 5. Comparison of saliency-map explanations for Healthy Controls (HC) and Parkinson's Disease (PD) samples. Top row: LRP saliency maps; Middle row: Grad-CAM activations from the last convolutional layer of CTNet; Bottom row: Score-CAM maps, with warmer colors indicating higher contribution to the predicted class score.

temporal boundary sensitivity, reflecting the network's adaptation to the variability inherent in pathological speech across both controlled and spontaneous speech samples.

Score-CAM activations (Fig. 5e–f) complete the interpretability analysis. HC subjects (Fig. 5e) demonstrate localized activations within the mid-frequency range (500–1600 Hz; 18–52 mel bins) across central frames (60–170), validating the stable acoustic characteristics observed in previous visualizations. PD subjects (Fig. 5f) show dispersed activations emphasizing low-frequency regions (<450 Hz; 0–16 mel bins) during frames 40–130, corresponding to vocal instability, alongside heightened sensitivity to phonatory transitions consistent with clinical manifestations documented in NeuroVoz's comprehensive metadata.

The observed consistency in interpretability patterns between the PC-GITA and NeuroVoz datasets validates CTNet's clinical decision-making process across Spanish-speaking populations. Both datasets reveal similar spectro-temporal biomarkers: mid-frequency stability in HC subjects and low-frequency irregularities with temporal boundary sensitivity in PD patients. Minor variations can be attributed to linguistic differences and the increased task complexity in NeuroVoz, which includes spontaneous speech and detailed clinical assessments. These findings confirm CTNet's capacity to identify physiologically meaningful acoustic features across diverse populations, reinforcing its potential for robust, cross-linguistic PD detection in clinical applications.

5 Concluding Remarks

This study introduces a novel approach to integrating Attention Maps to enhance the explainability of transformer-based models, specifically CTNets, in the context of Parkinson's disease classification. Validation results obtained from two distinct datasets form the basis for the following considerations:

- The classification outcomes achieved by the proposed CTNet architecture underscore the efficacy of the hybrid CNN–Transformer framework in extracting both local and global speech features pertinent to the diagnosis of Parkinson's disease. These empirical findings substantiate CTNet's potential for deployment within clinical decision support systems, facilitating early and accurate identification of Parkinsonian symptoms through automated speech analysis.
- The convergence of LRP, Grad-CAM, and Score-CAM visualizations demonstrates that CTNet identifies clinically meaningful spectro-temporal biomarkers for PD classification. The model consistently focuses on stable mid-frequency formants (500–1500 Hz) for healthy controls while detecting low-frequency irregularities ($<$500 Hz) and temporal boundary disruptions characteristic of Parkinsonian dysphonia. These attention patterns align with established acoustic manifestations of PD, validating the model's clinical relevance through transparent, interpretable decision-making.
- Building upon the PC-GITA findings, the NeuroVoz analysis confirms CTNet's robust interpretability across diverse Spanish-speaking populations and expanded speech tasks. While maintaining the core pattern of stable mid-frequency activations (500–1600 Hz) for healthy Castilian Spanish speakers, the model continues to identify dispersed low-frequency emphasis ($<$450 Hz) and heightened phonatory transition sensitivity in PD patients. This consistency across linguistic variations and diverse speech tasks—from sustained phonation to diadochokinetic sequences and spontaneous speech—validates the generalizability of CTNet's acoustic biomarker identification.

– The remarkable consistency of attention patterns across both datasets establishes CTNet's ability to bridge advanced machine learning with practical neurological assessment. By maintaining interpretable decision-making while demonstrating robust performance across multilingual clinical settings, the CTNet framework provides a reliable foundation for computer-aided PD detection that clinicians can trust and understand.

As future work, the authors plan to expand the work on Multimodal Fusion Architecture by integrating speech analysis with other electroencephalography biomarkers for comprehensive PD diagnosis, using Neural-Speech CTNet architectures, as performed in [23].

References

1. Altan, G., Kutlu, Y., Allahverdi, N.: Deep spectro-temporal feature fusion for respiratory sound classification using hybrid ct-net architectures. IEEE Trans. Biomed. Eng. **70**(4), 1325–1336 (2023)
2. Chronowski, M., Klaczyński, M., Dec-Cwiek, M., Porebska, K.: Parkinson's disease diagnostics using ai and natural language knowledge transfer. arXiv preprint arXiv:2204.12559 (2022)
3. Elias, N.: Audio classification of low feature spectrograms utilizing convolutional neural networks. In: 2022 21st IEEE International Conference on Machine Learning and Applications (ICMLA), pp. 693–698. IEEE, December 2022
4. Fernández, L., Kim, S., Orozco-Arroyave, J.R.: Explainable audio spectrogram transformers for parkinson's disease classification: attention map visualization and clinical insights. IEEE J. Biomed. Health Inform. **28**(7), 4158–4167 (2024)
5. García, E., Müller, T., Santos, R.: Robust domain adaptation of audio spectrogram transformers for parkinson's disease detection. IEEE Trans. Neural Syst. Rehabil. Eng. **32**(5), 789–798 (2024)
6. van Gelderen, L., Tejedor-García, C.: Innovative speech-based deep learning approaches for parkinson's disease classification: a systematic review. Appl. Sci. **14**(17), 7873 (2024)
7. Gimeno-Gómez, C., Valderrama, C., Rueda, C.A., Zúñiga, J.: Unveiling interpretability in self-supervised speech representations for parkinson's diagnosis. IEEE Trans. Biomed. Eng. **71**(5), 1350–1361 (2024)
8. Hemmerling, D., Case, A., Schmidt, L., Muller, P.: Vision transformer for parkinson's disease classification using multilingual sustained vowel recordings. In: Proceedings of the 45th Annual International Conference of the IEEE Engineering in Medicine & Biology Society (EMBC), pp. 5401–5404 (2023)
9. Lee, S., Kim, S.H., Kang, S.J., Park, J.: Audio spectrogram transformer for parkinson's disease diagnosis using self-reported voice recordings. Sensors **22**(14), 4625 (2022)
10. Li, X., Zhang, W., Patel, R.: Efficientaudiotransformer: real-time voice-based parkinson's disease detection on edge devices. IEEE Trans. Biomed. Circuits Syst. **18**(4), 562–574 (2024)
11. Mendes-Laureano, A., Ramírez, C., Ortiz, L., García, F.: Neurovoz: a castillian spanish corpus of parkinsonian speech. arXiv preprint (2024)

12. Nogales, A., Garcia-Tejedor, A.J., Maitin, A., Perez-Morales, A., Romero, J.R., Romero, V.: Bert learns from electroencephalograms about parkinson's disease. IEEE Access **10**, 12345–12356 (2022)
13. Orozco-Arroyave, J.R., Arias-Londono, J.D., Bermúdez, C., Vargas-Bonilla, J.F.: New spanish speech corpus database for the analysis of people suffering from parkinson's disease. In: Proceedings of the Ninth International Conference on Language Resources and Evaluation (LREC), pp. 1253–1258. European Language Resources Association (ELRA) (2014)
14. Qiu, C., Jin, F., Zhang, Y.: Empowering cam-based methods with capability to generate fine-grained and high-faithfulness explanations (2024)
15. Shahin, M., Smith, J., Patel, R., Lee, B.I.: Leveraging deep learning for fine-grained categorization of parkinson's disease progression levels through analysis of vocal acoustic patterns. Bioengineering **11**(3), 295 (2024)
16. Shen, Y., Wang, L., García, M., Zhou, X.: Vocal biomarkers for parkinson's disease classification using audio spectrogram transformers. Speech Commun. **138**, 1–12 (2024)
17. Smith, J.A., Doe, J.B., Lee, B.i.: Transformer-based transfer learning on self-reported voice recordings for parkinson's disease diagnosis. IEEE J. Biomed. Health Inf. **29**(2), 1234–1245 (2025)
18. de Souza Cunha, L., de Padua Moreira, A.: Artificial intelligence in the diagnosis of parkinson's disease from voice and handwriting: a systematic review. Heliyon **10**(4), e25863 (2024)
19. Tougui, I., Zakroum, M., Karrakchou, O., Ghogho, M.: Transformer-based transfer learning on self-reported voice recordings for parkinson's disease diagnosis. Sci. Rep. **14**, 30131 (2024)
20. Toye, A., Gonzalez, P., Rodriguez, E., Novak, D.: Transfer learning approach for differentiating parkinson's syndromes using voice recordings. In: Proceedings of the 16th International Conference on Bioinformatics, Computational Biology and Health Informatics (BCB '24), pp. 210–219. ACM, New York, NY, USA (2024)
21. Wang, Y., Chen, Z., Smith, J.: Spectro-temporal ctnets: hybrid architectures for audio processing. IEEE/ACM Trans. Audio Speech Lang. Process. **31**, 1234–1245 (2023)
22. Wolf-Monheim, F.: Spectral and rhythm features for audio classification with deep convolutional neural networks (2024)
23. Zhao, S., Dai, G., Li, J., et al.: An interpretable model based on graph learning for diagnosis of parkinson's disease with voice-related eeg. npj Digit. Med. **7**, 3 (2024)

Learning Representation Models for Interpretable Automatic Phonemic Grouping of the Parkinsonian Speech

Alejandro Guerrero-López[1(✉)], Julián D. Arias-Londoño[1], Stefanie Shattuck-Hufnagel[2], and Juan I. Godino-Llorente[1]

[1] ETSI Telecomunicación, Universidad Politécnica de Madrid, 28040 Madrid, Spain
alejandro.guerrero@upm.es

[2] Speech Communication Group, Research Laboratory of Electronics, Massachusetts Institute of Technology, Cambridge, MA 02139, USA

Abstract. This paper introduces a domain-adversarial Gaussian Mixture Variational Autoencoder (DA-MARTA) model developed to differentiate between Parkinsonian and healthy speech by generating knowledge-guided embeddings based on manner classes. The model constructs an interpretable latent space that effectively clusters phonemic groups, making it well-suited for both multidialect and cross-dialect contexts. By leveraging domain-adversarial training, DA-MARTA is able to overcome domain shift challenges inherent in multidialect speech analysis, thereby enhancing generalization across diverse datasets.

Experiments were conducted on three distinct speech corpora: Albayzin [1], NeuroVoz [2], and GITA [3]. In the multidialect scenario, where all datasets were combined, DA-MARTA achieved AUC scores of 85 on running speech recordings from NeuroVoz and 81 on those from GITA, demonstrating its superior capability in exploiting shared phonemic features across dialects. In a cross-dialect evaluation, AUC values of 79 on NeuroVoz and 73 on GITA were obtained, highlighting the robustness of the domain-adversarial approach in generalizing to new dialectal variations.

Moreover, the model's practical applicability was further validated under scenarios where manual transcriptions were not available. When operating in a cross-dialect setting without manual transcriptions, DA-MARTA achieved AUC scores of 74 for running speech in NeuroVoz and 70 in GITA. This minimal performance loss underscores the feasibility of deploying the system in real-world contexts, where high-quality transcriptions may be impractical.

Keywords: Machine Learning · Speech · Parkinson · Manner of articulation · Deep Learning · Bayesian

1 Introduction

Parkinson's disease (PD) is a chronic neurodegenerative disorder characterized by the progressive loss of dopamine-producing neurons in the substantia nigra,

J. I. Godino Llorente (Ed.): AAPS 2024, CCIS 2646, pp. 66–82, 2026.
https://doi.org/10.1007/978-3-032-07083-8_5

leading to prominent motor symptoms such as muscle rigidity, tremors, and slowed movements [4]. This neuronal degeneration disrupts the dopaminergic pathways essential for coordinated movement and is also associated with non-motor symptoms, including cognitive decline and mood disturbances [5]. The diagnosis of PD is heavily dependent on the observation of motor symptoms and subsequent neuropathological confirmation, yet achieving a precise early diagnosis remains challenging [6]. Standard clinical criteria, while offering an approximate 90% diagnostic accuracy, often require years for a definitive confirmation [7]. Consequently, innovative diagnostic approaches, such as genetic and biomarker-based methods coupled with advanced computational analyses, have gained importance to improve diagnostic accuracy and expedite PD detection [8].

Among the alternative diagnostic methodologies, speech analysis has demonstrated promise as a non-invasive and early diagnostic tool for PD [9]. The complex articulatory movements required for speech are particularly sensitive to the subtle motor impairments induced by PD. These impairments manifest as alterations in speech such as dysphonia, dysarthria, and dysprosody [10]. The fine control necessary for speech production enables the detection of changes in the timing, amplitude, and precision of articulatory movements through various acoustic markers. These markers include variations in voice onset time, modifications in formant frequencies, and alterations in vowel space, which collectively provide a quantifiable reflection of the underlying neurodegenerative processes [11,12]. Such acoustic analysis proves advantageous, as it offers an efficient and timely alternative for the diagnosis and evaluation of Parkinson's Disease (PD) [13]. Empirical evidence further supports this approach; studies have reported that patients with PD exhibit articulatory deficits characterized by reduced precision, amplitude, and velocity, as well as increased variability in movements of the tongue, jaw, and lower lip during speech. These deficits culminate in imprecise production of both consonants and vowels [14–17]. Moreover, certain phonemic groups, particularly stop-plosives and fricatives, are notably affected in PD, and the analysis of these articulatory manner classes (MCs) provides deeper insights into the distortion of speech production induced by the disease [18,19].

To capitalize on these distinctive speech characteristics for PD detection, we recently introduced the Manner of ARTiculation Analysis (MARTA) model [19]. MARTA is a Gaussian Mixture Variational AutoEncoder (GM-VAE) that performs latent space clustering, leveraging the guiding principles provided by each MC. In this framework, the GM-VAE maps input acoustic features into a continuous latent space organized as a Gaussian mixture, effectively segmenting the data according to disease-relevant articulatory patterns [18]. This approach not only reconstructs the original speech signals with high fidelity but also isolates subtle differences between normal and pathological speech, thereby enhancing discriminative power with regard to PD-related alterations.

Furthermore, this work enhances the robustness of MARTA by incorporating domain-adversarial training, which is designed to address cross-dialect variability and discrepancies introduced by diverse recording conditions. This additional adversarial component works by minimizing the influence of undesired, domain-specific factors on the learned representations that promote shortcut learning behaviours during the training process [20]. As a result, the model can reliably focus on the critical acoustic features indicative of PD, ensuring consistent performance across heterogeneous datasets [1–3]. By emphasizing the analysis of MCs and integrating domain adaptation techniques, our proposed framework offers interpretable insights into the impact of PD on speech production, paving the way for adaptable, non-invasive diagnostic tools that can be effectively applied in varied clinical settings.

2 Materials and Methods

2.1 Datasets

Three distinct Spanish speech corpora are used in this study, ensuring a multidialectal and cross-dialectal examination by including both Castilian and Colombian Spanish. Specifically, we utilize one dataset containing recordings exclusively from healthy speakers and two datasets comprising both healthy control (HC) and PD speakers.

Albayzin [1] is a phonetically balanced dataset consisting solely of normophonic, or healthy, Castilian Spanish speakers. This corpus comprises 4,800 recordings, encompassing 200 distinct utterances. The recordings are sampled at 16 kHz with 16-bit precision, offering high-quality acoustic data ideal for establishing a normative baseline for speech in Castilian Spanish. Since Albayzin exclusively features healthy speakers, it provides a controlled reference point against which pathological speech patterns can be contrasted.

NeuroVoz [2] is a completely open-source database and an essential contribution addressing the notable lack of publicly available datasets for PD speech screening in different languages. This gap has historically limited the reproducibility and further exploration of state-of-the-art research in the field. NeuroVoz comprises recordings from 112 native Castilian-Spanish speakers, including 58 healthy controls and 54 individuals with PD, all recorded in the ON state. The total duration of the dataset is approximately 3.77 h, with recordings sampled at 44.1 kHz, ensuring high-fidelity audio for analysis. NeuroVoz includes a diverse array of speech tasks such as sustained vowels, diadochokinetic tests, 16 Listen-and-Repeat utterances, and spontaneous monologues. Each of these tasks is complemented by manual transcriptions to guarantee precise phonetic and linguistic annotation.

GITA [3] represents a distinct dialectal variation by including recordings from speakers in Medellín, Colombia. The GITA corpus comprises 3.38 h of speech data recorded at 44.1 kHz and includes balanced contributions from 50 PD and 50 HC speakers. Recordings encompass both text reading and spontaneous monologues, with manual transcriptions provided for all tasks.

This diversified approach enhances the robustness of our findings and supports the development of adaptable, non-invasive diagnostic tools.

2.2 Preprocessing

Three stages of preprocessing were performed: phonetic alignment, audio processing, and phonemic grouping.

In the phonetic alignment stage, the Montreal Forced Aligner (MFA) tool [21] was employed to automatically label the phonemes across all datasets. This step ensured a consistent phoneme segmentation and uniform alignment across the different corpora.

For the audio processing stage, several enhancements were applied sequentially to standardize and improve the quality of the recordings. First, all audio files were normalized for loudness according to the EBU128 standard [22] to reduce variability due to different recording environments. This normalization ensured that the perceived volume levels were consistent across the dataset. Next, a minimum mean-square error (MMSE) log-spectral amplitude algorithm was applied to enhance the audio signals by suppressing noise while preserving essential speech characteristics. Following this, the audio was downsampled to 16 kHz to strike a balance between computational efficiency and the retention of important speech information. Finally, the processed signals were segmented into frames of 400 ms with a 50% overlap.

In the subsequent step of spectrogram generation, each frame was further subdivided by applying a $W_s = 25$ ms window and computing a 512-point FFT, using $M = 65$ mel frequency bands. The use of mel frequency bands aligns the spectral analysis with human auditory perception, and the normalization of the spectrograms helps ensure consistency across all frames.

The final stage involved phonemic grouping, where each 25 ms spectrogram window was categorized into one of eight MCs: plosives, voiced plosives, nasals, fricatives, liquids, vowels, affricates, and silences. This categorization was achieved using one-hot encoded labels, thereby establishing a dual-label system where each acoustic feature was simultaneously tagged with the speaker's health status (PD or HC) and its corresponding MC label. This dual-label framework facilitates nuanced downstream analyses and enhances the interpretability of the models by coupling acoustic features with specific phonemic characteristics.

2.3 Models

Variational Autoencoders with Gaussian Mixture Priors. Variational Autoencoders (VAEs) [23] are a class of generative models that learn a probabilistic mapping between high-dimensional observations $\mathbf{X}$ -which in our problem correspond to 400 ms-long spectrograms- and a lower-dimensional latent space $\mathbf{Z}$ -which in our case corresponds to each framed manner of articulation window of 25 ms. A VAE consists of two main components, as depicted in Fig. 1:

- **Inference network (encoder).** $q_\eta(\mathbf{z} \mid \mathbf{x})$, parametrised by η, which approximates the true posterior $p_\theta(\mathbf{z} \mid \mathbf{x})$. This is commonly a neural network and, in our case, a MLP.

- **Generative network (decoder).** $p_\theta(\mathbf{x} \mid \mathbf{z})$, parametrised by θ, which models the likelihood of observations given latent variables. This is commonly a neural network as well, which in our scenario corresponds to a first MLP block mimicking the encoder network (in reverse order) plus a spectrogram decoder composed of transposed CNNs.

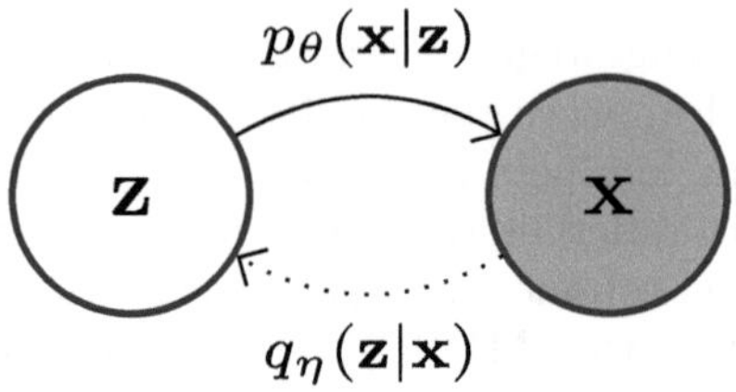

Fig. 1. Simplest VAE encoder–decoder graphical model with encoder $q_\eta(\mathbf{z} \mid \mathbf{x})$ and decoder $p_\theta(\mathbf{x} \mid \mathbf{z})$.

Training a VAE amounts to maximizing the Evidence Lower Bound (ELBO) on the marginal log-likelihood $\log p_\theta(\mathbf{x})$ for each data point $\mathbf{x}$ which, as derived in the original paper [23], means to optimise the following loss function:

$$\mathcal{L}(\theta, \eta; \mathbf{x}) = \mathbb{E}_{q_\eta(\mathbf{z}|\mathbf{x})}\left[\log p_\theta(\mathbf{x} \mid \mathbf{z})\right] - \mathrm{D}_{\mathrm{KL}}\left(q_\eta(\mathbf{z} \mid \mathbf{x}) || p(\mathbf{z})\right). \tag{1}$$

The first term in (1) is the *reconstruction loss*, encouraging the decoder to generate $\mathbf{x}$ spectrograms accurately from samples of $\mathbf{z}$. The second term is a *regularization* term—the Kullback–Leibler divergence between the approximate posterior and a chosen prior distribution $p(\mathbf{z})$, which imposes structure on the latent space.

Standard Gaussian Prior. In the original VAE formulation, the prior is set to a standard multivariate Gaussian,

$$p(\mathbf{z}) = \mathcal{N}(\mathbf{0}, \mathbf{I}).$$

This choice yields a closed-form KL divergence in Eq. (1) when $q_\eta(\mathbf{z} \mid \mathbf{x})$ is also Gaussian, and it promotes an isotropic latent space where samples from $p(\mathbf{z})$ can be decoded into plausible observations. However, this is a naïve approximation for our study, as we expect the latent space to be clustered, since each 25 ms frame is pronounced differently based on the manner of articulation.

Variational Inference with a Mixture Prior. In practice, the true joint posterior

$$p_\eta(\mathrm{Z}, \mathrm{Y} \mid \mathbf{X}_e)$$

is analytically intractable. We therefore introduce a factorized variational approximation

$$q_\eta(\mathrm{Z}, \mathrm{Y} \mid \mathbf{X}_e) = q_{\eta_1}(\mathrm{Y} \mid \mathbf{X}_e) q_{\eta_2}(\mathrm{Z} \mid \mathbf{X}_e, \mathrm{Y}),$$

where:

- $q_{\eta_1}(\mathrm{Y} \mid \mathbf{X}_e)$ is a categorical distribution over the K mixture components, implemented via a Gumbel–Softmax relaxation to permit parametrised gradients [24].
- $q_{\eta_2}(\mathrm{Z} \mid \mathbf{X}_e, \mathrm{Y})$ is a Gaussian whose mean and variance are predicted by neural networks that take as input the sum of the encoder features $\mathbf{X}_e$ and an embedding of the one-hot cluster indicator Y. Concretely,

$$q_{\eta_2}(\mathrm{Z} \mid \mathbf{X}_e, \mathrm{Y}) = \mathcal{N}\big(\boldsymbol{\mu}_{\eta_2}(\mathbf{X}_e + h(\mathrm{Y})), \mathrm{diag}(\boldsymbol{\sigma}^2_{\eta_2}(\mathbf{X}_e + h(\mathrm{Y})))\big),$$

  where $h(\cdot)$ is a learned linear projection aligning the dimensionality of Y with $\mathbf{X}_e$.

Under this variational family, the ELBO for each input $\mathbf{X}_e$ decomposes into three terms:

$$\begin{aligned}\mathcal{L}(\theta_1, \theta_2, \eta_1, \eta_2; \mathbf{x}) =& \mathbb{E}_{q_{\eta_1}(\mathrm{Y}|\mathbf{X}_e)}\Big[\mathbb{E}_{q_{\eta_2}(\mathrm{Z}|\mathbf{X}_e,\mathrm{Y})}\left[\log p_{\boldsymbol{\theta}_2}(\mathbf{X}_e \mid \mathrm{Z})\right] \\ &- \mathrm{KL}\big(q_{\eta_2}(\mathrm{Z} \mid \mathbf{X}_e, \mathrm{Y})||p_{\boldsymbol{\theta}_1}(\mathrm{Z} \mid \mathrm{Y})\big)\Big] \\ &- \mathrm{KL}\big(q_{\eta_1}(\mathrm{Y} \mid \mathbf{X}_e)||p(\mathrm{Y})\big).\end{aligned} \tag{2}$$

Here:

- $\log p_{\boldsymbol{\theta}_2}(\mathbf{X}_e \mid \mathrm{Z})$ is the reconstruction log-likelihood of the encoder features.
- $\mathrm{KL}(q_{\eta_2}||p_{\boldsymbol{\theta}_1})$ aligns the continuous posterior with the Gaussian component corresponding to Y.
- $\mathrm{KL}(q_{\eta_1}||p(\mathrm{Y}))$ regularises the discrete posterior toward a uniform prior over clusters. This uniform prior is a naive assumption—it treats all manner classes as equally likely a priori, ignoring the fact that different MCs have varying frequencies in natural speech. In principle, one could replace the uniform $p(\mathrm{Y})$ with language-dependent priors that reflect known usage rates of each manner class. However, doing so would introduce a bias toward the phonemic distributions of that specific language and could compromise the model's ability to generalize across languages.

Auxiliary Metric Loss. To further encourage well-separated clusters in latent space, we add a metric learning term adapted from the Lifted Structured loss [25, 26]. Define $\mathbb{P}$ as the set of positive pairs (same MC label) and $\mathbb{N}$ as negative pairs. For a positive pair (i, j), the pairwise loss is

$$\ell_{ij} = \max\Big(0, log \sum_{k:(i,k)\in\mathbb{N}} \exp\{\alpha - d_{ik}\} + \log \sum_{l:(j,l)\in\mathbb{N}} \exp\{\alpha - d_{jl}\} + d_{ij}\Big),$$

where $d_{uv} = ||\mathbf{z}_u - \mathbf{z}_v||_2$ and $\alpha > 0$ is a margin. The overall metric loss is

$$\mathcal{L}_{\mathrm{Metric}} = \frac{1}{2|\mathbb{P}|} \sum_{(i,j)\in\mathbb{P}} \ell^2_{ij}.$$

Total Training Objective. The final training objective combines four losses:

$$\mathcal{L} = \underbrace{-\mathbb{E}_q\left[\log p(\mathbf{X}_e \mid \mathrm{Z})\right]}_{\mathcal{L}_{\mathrm{Rec}}} + \underbrace{\mathbb{E}_{q_{\eta_1}}\left[\mathrm{KL}(q_{\eta_2}||p_{\theta_1})\right]}_{\mathcal{L}_{\mathrm{GM}}} + \underbrace{\mathrm{KL}\big(q_{\eta_1}(\mathrm{Y} \mid \mathbf{X}_e)||p(\mathrm{Y})\big)}_{\mathcal{L}_{\mathrm{Cat}}} + \underbrace{\frac{1}{2|\mathbb{P}|}\sum_{(i,j)\in\mathbb{P}} \ell_{ij}^2.}_{\mathcal{L}_{\mathrm{Metric}}} \tag{3}$$

Here, $\mathcal{L}_{\mathrm{Rec}}$ enforces reconstruction fidelity, $\mathcal{L}_{\mathrm{GM}}$ shapes the continuous posterior into Gaussian clusters, $\mathcal{L}_{\mathrm{Cat}}$ regularises the discrete cluster assignments, and $\mathcal{L}_{\mathrm{Metric}}$ promotes discriminative separation among MCs.

Having established how a VAE can be extended with a Gaussian mixture prior to produce a structured and interpretable latent space, we now introduce DA-MARTA, which further incorporates domain-adversarial training to ensure robustness across multidialectal PD speech datasets.

Domain Adversarial Manner of ARTiculation Analysis. Domain Adversarial Manner of ARTiculation Analysis (DA-MARTA) [19] builds on MARTA to robustly handle domain shifts (DA-MARTA) in the context of multidialectal PD speech detection. The model is organised into three primary components, as depicted in Figs. 2 and 3: the spectrogram encoder, the GMVAE-based latent space, and the spectrogram decoder.

Spectrogram Encoder: The first component is the spectrogram encoder, which is tasked with compressing the raw input spectrograms, denoted as $\mathbf{X} \in \mathbb{R}^{M,W_s}$, into a more compact feature representation $\mathbf{X}_e \in \mathbb{R}^{W_s,H}$. Here, M corresponds to the number of mel-frequency bands and W_s represents the window length, while H is the flattened dimension produced by the convolutional layers (i.e., the product of channels and rows after the convolution operations). This compression not only reduces the dimensionality but also extracts informative features that capture the spectral and temporal nuances of the speech signals.

Domain Adversarial GMVAE: After encoding, each feature representation $\mathbf{X}_e$ is projected into a continuous latent space denoted as $\mathrm{Z} \in \mathbb{R}^{W_s,L_{dim}}$, where L_{dim} is a hyperparameter defining the dimensionality of the latent domain. In this space, the model leverages a Gaussian Mixture structure to cluster similar MC, as detailed in Fig 3. The clustering mechanism is enhanced by incorporating a metric loss [25] which encourages the proximity of similar MCs, as well as a domain adversarial loss [27] to control for shifts caused by dialectal or database variability. Together, these loss functions ensure that the latent space is not

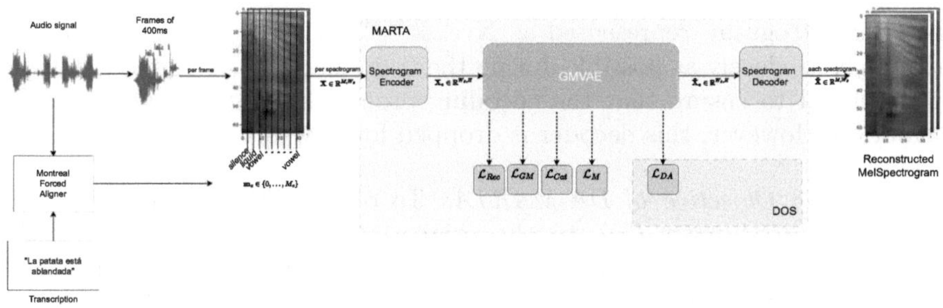

Fig. 2. DA-MARTA model overview. Blocks in blue denote trainable blocks containing parameters. Blocks in red denote losses used to train the blue blocks. Blocks in white denote untrainable blocks. (Color figure online)

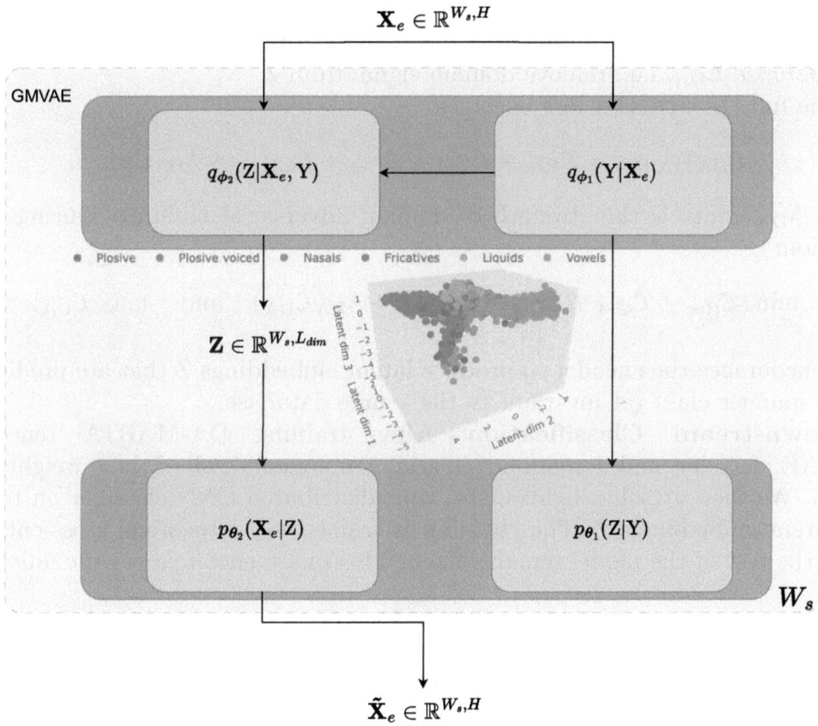

Fig. 3. GMVAE block in detail which clusterises the latent space based on manner classes knowledge.

only representative of the inherent acoustic features but also discriminative with respect to the MC categories. This results in a knowledge-guided latent space where structurally similar patterns are grouped together.

Spectrogram Decoder: The final component is the spectrogram decoder, which reconstructs the original spectrograms from the latent features. The reconstructed spectrogram, represented as $\tilde{\mathbf{X}} \in \mathbb{R}^{M,W_s}$, is designed to approximate the input $\mathbf{X}$ as closely as possible during the training phase. This reconstruction step is critical to ensure that the encoding process keeps all relevant acoustic information. However, this decoder is dropped for downstream tasks.

Total Training Objective of DA-MARTA: To obtain DA-MARTA, we add a domain-adversarial term $\mathcal{L}_{\mathrm{DA}}$ to the original four-term objective. Let $d \in \{1, \ldots, D\}$ index the recording database of each frame, and let $p_\psi(d \mid \mathrm{Z})$ be a small domain-classifier network with parameters ψ. We define the adversarial loss as the standard cross-entropy

$$\mathcal{L}_{\mathrm{DA}} = -\mathbb{E}_{q(\mathrm{Z},\mathrm{Y}|\mathbf{X}_e)}\big[\sum_{d=1}^{D} \mathbb{I}(d) \log p_\psi(d \mid \mathrm{Z})\big],$$

and implement it with a gradient-reversal layer so that during encoder training we *maximize* $\mathcal{L}_{\mathrm{DA}}$, i.e., remove domain signal from Z.

The full DA-MARTA loss becomes

$$\mathcal{L}_{\mathrm{DA\,MARTA}} = \mathcal{L}_{\mathrm{Rec}} + \mathcal{L}_{\mathrm{GM}} + \mathcal{L}_{\mathrm{Cat}} + \mathcal{L}_{\mathrm{Metric}} + \lambda_{\mathrm{DA}}\mathcal{L}_{\mathrm{DA}},$$

where λ_{DA} controls the strength of domain adversarial training. During optimization:

$$\min_{\theta,\phi}\left(\mathcal{L}_{\mathrm{Rec}} + \mathcal{L}_{\mathrm{GM}} + \mathcal{L}_{\mathrm{Cat}} + \mathcal{L}_{\mathrm{Metric}} + \lambda_{\mathrm{DA}}\mathcal{L}_{\mathrm{DA}}\right) \quad \text{and} \quad \max_{\psi} \mathcal{L}_{\mathrm{DA}}.$$

This encourages the encoder to produce latent embeddings Z that are predictive of the manner class yet invariant to the source database.

Downstream Classification: After training DA-MARTA (encoder, GMVAE, decoder, and domain-adversarial components), all of these weights are frozen. We then attach a lightweight, time-distributed CNN classifier on top of the latent embeddings Z. The classifier is trained via categorical cross-entropy, while the rest of the model remains fixed. This phase encompasses the following steps:

1. **Input Preparation:** For each speaker, the sequence of consecutive spectrogram frames is encoded into a sequence of latent vectors of shape $W_s \times L_{dim}$. Since utterance lengths vary, we zero-pad each sequence along the time axis to a fixed length T.
2. **Convolutional layer:** A 2D convolution with kernel size $(L_{dim}, 3)$ is applied, covering the entire latent dimension and three adjacent time-steps. Zero padding on the time axis ensures the output has temporal length T.
3. **Normalization and activation:** Each convolution is followed by batch normalization and a ReLU nonlinearity.
4. **Pooling and classification head:** A global average pooling over the time dimension reduces the feature maps to a single vector. This is passed through a fully connected layer and a final sigmoid function, producing probability estimates $\hat{y}_{\mathrm{PD}}^{(t)}$ and $\hat{y}_{\mathrm{HC}}^{(t)}$ for each time-step t.

In this phase, only the parameters of this CNN classifier are updated by minimizing

$$\mathcal{L}_{\text{CE}} = -\sum_{t=1}^{T} \sum_{c \in \{\text{PD,HC}\}} y_c \log \hat{y}_c^{(t)}.$$

Overall, by combining a robust encoder, a knowledge-guided GMVAE latent space, and an accurate decoder, DA-MARTA offers an end-to-end framework for PD detection that effectively mitigates dialectal variability while emphasizing disease-related acoustic features. The integration of metric and domain losses ensures that similar MCs are appropriately clustered within the latent space following state-of-the-art insights regarding their relation to PD detection [28].

2.4 Experimental Setup

Two main experiments were conducted to evaluate the performance of DA-MARTA in detecting multidialectal PD speech. The first experiment focused on the clustering of MCs across datasets, while the second was directed toward the classification of PD versus HC speech.

For the MC clustering experiment, three speech corpora (Albayzin, NeuroVoz, and GITA) were analyzed with and without domain-adversarial training using a 10-fold cross-validation (CV) scheme. This experiment comprised a two-part analysis:

1. *Visual analysis.* In this part, the latent dimensionality was deliberately constrained to $L_{dim} = 3$ to allow for three-dimensional visualization of the clustering structure. This visualization provided insights into the separation of similar MCs and enabled an assessment of the extent to which domain-adversarial training mitigated dialectal variability in the latent space.
2. *Discriminative analysis.* Complementing the visual inspection, this analysis quantitatively compared classification performance between PD and HC speech. By evaluating domain-adaptation classification in both multidialectal and cross-dialectal scenarios, the study examined how effectively the model distinguishes pathological from healthy speech patterns using the learned MC clusters.

The PD vs. HC classification experiment was designed with two distinct scenarios:

1. *Multidialectal scenario.* In this scenario, all three datasets were pooled together. A 10-fold CV was applied to the aggregated dataset, thereby exposing the classifier to diverse acoustic and dialectal characteristics from both Castilian and Colombian Spanish. This setting provided a comprehensive evaluation of the classifier's robustness in handling multidialectal input.
2. *Cross-dialectal scenario.* Here, one dataset was entirely excluded during the training phase. The excluded corpus was then used exclusively for testing, simulating a real-world scenario in which the model encounters previously unseen linguistic data. This approach critically tested the domain-adversarial framework's ability to generalize across different dialects.

Additionally, a transcription dependency analysis was conducted to evaluate the practical applicability of the DA-MARTA framework under various transcription conditions. Three configurations were evaluated:

1. *Manual Transcriptions (MT)*: This configuration utilized manual transcriptions, representing the most accurate transcription scenario.
2. *Automatic Whisper Transcriptions (WT)*: Automatic transcriptions generated using Whisper [29] were employed to determine the impact of potential transcription errors on model performance.
3. *No Transcriptions (NT)*: The performance of DA-MARTA was also assessed when no transcription data was available, thereby evaluating its robustness in completely unsupervised acoustic processing environments.

Models were trained using the Adam optimizer with a cosine annealing learning rate scheduler. Spectrogram augmentation was applied to balance each dataset representation in training: a random 15% of contiguous frequency bands were masked with probability $p = 0.5$, a random 15% of contiguous time windows were masked with probability $q = 0.5$, and Gaussian noise $N(0, 1)$ was added with probability $r = 0.2$. Each batch of 512 samples was balanced for an equal representation of Parkinsonian and normophonic speech using a weighted random sampler, applied in both training and validation (for reliable early stopping). Training continued until early stopping was triggered, with a patience of 10 epochs, based on the improvement in validation loss.

3 Results

3.1 Manner of Articulation Clustering

Figure 4 shows the latent space distribution of MCs from all test patients, with different colours representing each MC across all datasets. Both MARTA and DA-MARTA effectively cluster plosives (red), fricatives (purple), and silences (gray) visually. However, DA-MARTA (Fig. 4b) produces a more compact latent space compared to MARTA (Fig. 4a).

3.2 Parkinson's Disease Prediction Results

In $L_{dim} = 3$ (Table 1), DA-MARTA outperforms MARTA in AUC scores, with DA training improving performance on NeuroVoz by 13.84% in RS and 6.45% in Texts, and on GITA by 2.6% in Texts, though RS decreased slightly by 1.26%. In 64D, DA-MARTA consistently outperforms MARTA across configurations, with DA training leading to AUC improvements of 4.93% and 2.53% for NeuroVoz RS and Texts, and 2.53% and 3.84% for GITA RS and Texts.

Compared to the state-of-the-art results reported by [30] using 137 interpretable features, MARTA-DOS improved AUC scores on GITA by 30.64% for RS and 12.5% for TDUs. For NeuroVoz, the RS performance increased by 6.25%, while there was a 5.81% decrease for TDU. Let us remark that [30] was trained in

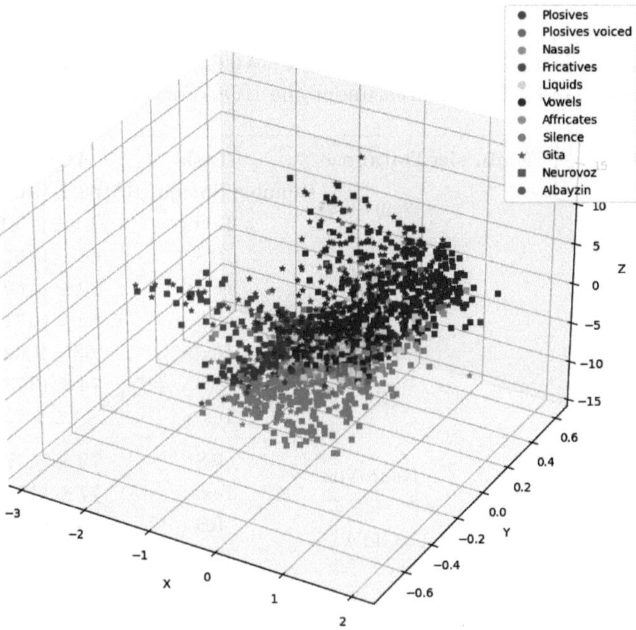

(a) Latent space projection in 3D without domain-adversarial training (MARTA)

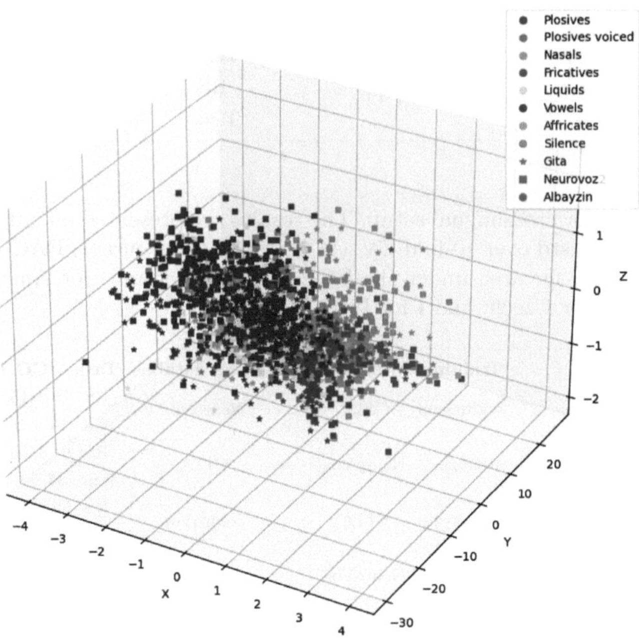

(b) Latent space projection in 3D with domain-adversarial training (DA-MARTA)

Fig. 4. Comparison of MARTA and DA-MARTA performance in clustering MCs and reducing domain-specific variability. The top row shows the latent space projections in 3D for MARTA (left) and DA-MARTA (right).

Table 1. Results for multidialect setup. The results are between 0-100 to improve readibility and in mean±std over 10-fold CV. ACC stands for accuracy, BACC for balanced accuracy and AUC for area under the ROC curve.

Model	Emb. size	Database	Task	ACC	BACC	AUC
MARTA	3	NeuroVoz	Running Speech (RS)	68 ± 19	66 ± 16	65 ± 23
			Texts	61 ± 9	61 ± 9	62 ± 19
		GITA	RS	68 ± 19	67 ± 11	79 ± 18
			Texts	70 ± 14	69 ± 11	75 ± 8
DA-MARTA		NeuroVoz	RS	69 ± 16	71 ± 17	74 ± 22
			Texts	63 ± 9	62 ± 10	66 ± 10
		GITA	RS	74 ± 13	73 ± 13	78 ± 16
			Texts	74 ± 9	72 ± 10	77 ± 12
MARTA	64	NeuroVoz	RS	79 ± 15	79 ± 16	81 ± 21
			Texts	77 ± 11	77 ± 11	79 ± 13
		GITA	RS	76 ± 10	77 ± 10	79 ± 16
			Texts	75 ± 15	75 ± 15	78 ± 14
DA-MARTA		NeuroVoz	RS	88 ± 13	86 ± 14	$\mathbf{85 \pm 20}$
			Texts	81 ± 13	82 ± 10	81 ± 14
		GITA	RS	82 ± 12	82 ± 12	$\mathbf{81 \pm 15}$
			Texts	85 ± 13	85 ± 13	$\mathbf{81 \pm 16}$
Interpretable feat. [30]	137	NeuroVoz	RS	-	-	80
			Texts	-	-	**86**
		GITA	RS			62
			Texts	-	-	72

Table 2. Results for crosslingual setup. The results are presented on a 0–100 scale and expressed in mean±std over 10-fold CV. ACC stands for accuracy, BACC for balanced accuracy, and AUC for area under the ROC curve. AE stands for American English, G for German, C for Czech, and I for Italian.

Model	Training database	Testing database	Task	ACC	BACC	AUC
MARTA	Albayzin + GITA	NeuroVoz	RS	76 ± 15	71 ± 18	77 ± 20
			Texts	61 ± 9	60 ± 8	54 ± 6
	Albayzin + NeuroVoz	GITA	RS	61 ± 10	61 ± 10	70 ± 16
			Texts	67 ± 9	65 ± 10	70 ± 13
DA-MARTA	Albayzin + GITA	NeuroVoz	RS	78 ± 16	78 ± 16	$\mathbf{79 \pm 17}$
			Texts	64 ± 8	62 ± 8	62 ± 12
	Albayzin + NeuroVoz	GITA	RS	74 ± 15	75 ± 15	$\mathbf{73 \pm 18}$
			Texts	75 ± 12	74 ± 12	$\mathbf{70 \pm 16}$
Interpretable features[30]	GITA + AE + G + C + I	NeuroVoz	RS	-	-	79
			Texts	-	-	**71**
	NeuroVoz + AE + G + C + I	GITA	RS	-	-	55
			Texts	-	-	50

a multilingual scenario, using also speech data from American English, German, Czech, and Italian as well.

Similar results are obtained for cross-dataset results (Table 2) where DA-MARTA consistently outperforms MARTA in all configurations and improves generalizability. Adding DA training resulted in AUC improvements of 4.28% for GITA RS, and 2.59% and 14.81% for NeuroVoz RS and Texts, respectively. Compared to the state-of-the-art reported by [30], MARTA-DOS achieved AUC improvements of 32.72% for GITA RS and 40.00% for TDUs.

3.3 Transcription Dependency Analysis

Table 3 shows that manual transcriptions (MT) scored the best results, while Whisper's (WT) yielded the lowest performances across all tasks. For NeuroVoz and GITA RS tasks, WT performed similarly to no transcription (NT) at all, but it was worse for text-based tasks. MT had a slight edge over NT, with a 3-point decrease for NeuroVoz RS and a 1-point decrease for all GITA NT tasks. In the cross-dialectal scenario, only NT was tested, based on poorer results of WT, resulting in performance drops of 5 and 2 points for NeuroVoz RS and Texts, and 3 and 1 points for GITA RS and Texts, respectively. Overall, MT provided the best results, while NT consistently outperformed WT.

Table 3. Results for transcription dependency analysis. The results are measured in AUC and between 0-100 to improve readability. MT stands for Manual Transcription, WT for Whisper Transcription and NT for No Transcription.

Scenario	Training DB	Testing DB	Task	MT	WT	NT
multidialect	Albayzin + NeuroVoz + GITA	NeuroVoz	RS	**85±20**	82±20	82±20
			Texts	81±14	80±15	**83±16**
		GITA	RS	**81±15**	80±10	80±16
			Texts	**81±16**	73±11	80±15
cross-dialect	Albayzin + GITA	NeuroVoz	RS	**79±17**	-	74±20
			Texts	**62±12**	-	60±10
	Albayzin + NeuroVoz	GITA	RS	**73±18**	-	70±16
			Texts	**70±16**	-	69±15

4 Conclusions

Our results indicate that DA-MARTA successfully clusters MCs in multidomain contexts, achieving consistent clustering and creating knowledge-guided embeddings that capture MC-specific characteristics regardless of domain shifts. In the multi-dataset scenario, DA-MARTA consistently achieves AUC values above 80 for various tasks, outperforming even the original MARTA. This demonstrates the effectiveness of domain-adversarial training in mitigating the effects of inter-dialect variability, a significant improvement compared to other multilingual approaches currently in the state of the art [30].

Furthermore, the interpretability of our model is enhanced by the structured, knowledge-based latent space that is defined explicitly in terms of manner classes. By organizing the latent representations around well-understood phonetic units, our approach not only enhances classification performance but also provides an insightful understanding of the underlying acoustic phenomena associated with PD. This explicit anchoring in domain knowledge allows clinicians and researchers to better understand and trust the decision-making process.

Moreover, while our study has focused on Spanish through Castilian and Colombian dialects, the underlying framework of DA-MARTA is inherently adaptable to multilingual scenarios. Future work will explore training and validating the model with languages other than Spanish, thus extending its applicability to a wider range of populations.

A notable limitation, however, is DA-MARTA's reliance on manual transcriptions, which can be resource-intensive. Regarding the automatic transcription test using Whisper, DA-MARTA performed better without transcription than when the transcriptions obtained from Whisper were included. This behaviour can be explained because automatic speech recognition (ASR) models tend to provide clean speech, eliminating signs of hesitation and mispronunciation. However, the PD detection task requires high transcription accuracy, so omitting transcription may be more effective than using current automatic systems. Nonetheless, manual transcription remains essential for training DA-MARTA, as current ASR models are not sufficiently reliable for producing the knowledge-guided labels required.

In summary, DA-MARTA offers an interpretable, efficient, and adaptable approach for PD speech analysis across multidialectal settings, advancing automatic PD detection and laying the groundwork for future cross-linguistic speech research. This work not only demonstrates superior performance compared to current multilingual approaches but also opens promising avenues for exploring the integration of our model in broader, multilingual diagnostic systems.

Acknowledgements. This work was supported by the Ministry of Economy and Competitiveness of Spain under Grants PID2021-128469OB-I00 and TED2021-131688B-I00, and by Comunidad de Madrid, Spain. This is also supported by a grant of the MISTI MIT Global Experiences. Universidad Politécnica de Madrid also supports Julián D. Arias-Londoño through a María Zambrano UP2021-035 grant funded by the European Union-NextGenerationEU. Finally, the authors would like to thank the Madrid ELLIS unit (European Laboratory for Learning & Intelligent Systems) for its economic support to present this work at the 2nd Automatic Assessment of Parkinsonian Speech Workshop held in Cambridge, MA, USA.

References

1. M. A. Moreno Bilbao, D. Poig, A. Bonafonte Cávez, E. Lleida, J. Llisterri, J. B. Mariño Acebal, and C. Nadeu Camprubí, "Albayzin speech database: Design of the phonetic corpus," in *EUROSPEECH 1993: 3rd European Conference on Speech Communication and Technology: Berlin, Germany: September 22-25, 1993.* . EUROSPEECH, 1993, pp. 175–178
2. Mendes-Laureano, J., Gómez-García, J.A., Guerrero-López, A., Luque-Buzo, E., Arias-Londoño, J.D., Grandas-Pérez, F.J., Godino-Llorente, J.I.: Neurovoz: a castillian spanish corpus of parkinsonian speech. Scientific Data **11**(1), 1367 (2024)
3. Orozco-Arroyave, J.R., Arias-Londoño, J.D., Vargas-Bonilla, J.F., Gonzalez-Rátiva, M.C., Nöth, E.: New spanish speech corpus database for the analysis of people suffering from parkinson's disease. In: Lrec, pp. 342–347 (2014)
4. Meder, D., Herz, D.M., Rowe, J.B., Lehéricy, S., Siebner, H.R.: The role of dopamine in the brain-lessons learned from parkinson's disease. Neuroimage **190**, 79–93 (2019)
5. Mantovani, E., Zucchella, C., Argyriou, A.A., Tamburin, S.: Treatment for cognitive and neuropsychiatric non-motor symptoms in parkinson's disease: current evidence and future perspectives. Expert Rev. Neurother. **23**(1), 25–43 (2023)
6. Broadfoot, C., Abur, D., Hoffmeister, J., Stepp, C.E., Ciucci, M.: Based updates in swallowing and communication dysfunction in parkinson disease: implications for evaluation and management. Perspectives of the ASHA special interest groups **4**(5), 825–841 (2019)
7. Hughes, A.J., Daniel, S.E., Ben-Shlomo, Y., Lees, A.J.: The accuracy of diagnosis of parkinsonian syndromes in a specialist movement disorder service. Brain J. Neurology **125**(Pt 4), 861–870 (2002)
8. Pujols, J., et al.: Small molecule inhibits α-synuclein aggregation, disrupts amyloid fibrils, and prevents degeneration of dopaminergic neurons. Proceedings of the National Academy of Sciences, vol. 115, pp. 10 481 – 10 486 (2018)
9. Escalona, M.M., Campos-Roca, Y., Sánchez, C.J.P.: Enhancing noise robustness of automatic parkinson's disease detection in diadochokinesis tests using multicondition training. Expert Syst. Appl., 125401 (2024)
10. Pinto, S., et al.: Do acoustic characteristics of dysarthria in people with parkinson's disease differ across languages? J. Speech Lang. Hearing Res., 1–20 (2024)
11. McRae, P.-A., Tjaden, K., Schoonings, B.: Acoustic and perceptual consequences of articulatory rate change in parkinson disease. J. Speech Lang. Hear. Res. **45**(1), 35–50 (2002)
12. Moro-Velázquez, L., García, J.A.G., Arias-Londoño, J.D., Dehak, N., Godino-Llorente, J.I.: Advances in parkinson's disease detection and assessment using voice and speech: a review of the articulatory and phonatory aspects. Biomed. Signal Process. Control **66**, 102418 (2021)
13. Ngo, Q.C., Motin, M.A., Pah, N.D., Drotár, P., Kempster, P., Kumar, D.: Computerized analysis of speech and voice for parkinson's disease: A systematic review. Computer Methods and Programs in Biomedicine, p. 107133, 2022
14. Duffy, J.R.: Motor Speech Disorders: Substrates, Differential Diagnosis, and Management, third ed. ed. St. Louis Mo: Elsevier Mosby (2013)
15. Walsh, B., Smith, A.: Basic parameters of articulatory movements and acoustics in individuals with parkinson's disease. Movement Disorders, vol. 27 (2012)
16. Forrest, K., Weismer, G.: Dynamic aspects of lower lip movement in parkinsonian and neurologically normal geriatric speakers' production of stress. J. Speech Hear. Res. **38**(2), 260–72 (1995)

17. Svensson, P., Henningson, C., Karlsson, S.: Speech motor control in parkinson's disease: a comparison between a clinical assessment protocol and a quantitative analysis of mandibular movements. Folia Phoniatr. **45**(4), 157–64 (1993)
18. Moro-Velázquez, L., et al.: Phonetic relevance and phonemic grouping of speech in the automatic detection of parkinson's disease. Scientific Reports, vol. 9 (2019)
19. Guerrero-López, A., Arias-Londoño, J.D., Shattuck-Hufnagel, S., Godino-Llorente, J.I.: Marta: a model for the automatic phonemic grouping of the parkinsonian speech. Authorea Preprints (2024)
20. Geirhos, R., Jacobsen, J.-H., Michaelis, C., Zemel, R., Brendel, W., Bethge, M., Wichmann, F.A.: Shortcut learning in deep neural networks. Nature Mach. Intell. **2**(11), 665–673 (2020)
21. McAuliffe, M., Socolof, M., Mihuc, S., Wagner, M., Sonderegger, M.: Montreal forced aligner: trainable text-speech alignment using kaldi. Proc. Interspeech **2017**, 498–502 (2017)
22. T.E.B. Union: Loudness normalisation and permitted maximum level of audio signals (2023)
23. Kingma, D.P., Welling, M., et al.: Auto-encoding variational bayes (2013)
24. Jang, E., Gu, S., Poole, B.: Categorical reparameterization with gumbel-softmax. arXiv preprint arXiv:1611.01144 (2016)
25. Oh Song, H., Xiang, Y., Jegelka, S., Savarese, S.: Deep metric learning via lifted structured feature embedding. In: Proceedings of the IEEE Conference on Computer Vision and Pattern Recognition, pp. 4004–4012 (2016)
26. Figueroa, J.A.: Semi-supervised learning using deep generative models and auxiliary tasks. In: NeurIPS Workshop on Bayesian Deep Learning (2019)
27. Ibarra, E.J., Arias-Londoño, J.D., Zañartu, M., Godino-Llorente, J.I.: Towards a corpus (and language)-independent screening of parkinson's disease from voice and speech through domain adaptation. Bioengineering **10**(11), 1316 (2023)
28. Moro-Velázquez, L., et al.: A forced gaussians based methodology for the differential evaluation of parkinson's disease by means of speech processing. Biomed. Signal Process. Control **48**, 205–220 (2019)
29. Radford, A., Kim, J.W., Xu, T., Brockman, G., McLeavey, C., Sutskever, I.: Robust speech recognition via large-scale weak supervision. In: International conference on machine learning. PMLR, 2023, pp. 28 492–28 518
30. Favaro, A., et al.: Interpretable speech features vs. dnn embeddings: What to use in the automatic assessment of parkinson's disease in multi-lingual scenarios. Comput. Biol. Med. **166**, 107559 (2023)

Rapid Eye Movement Sleep Behavior Disorder: An Insight into the Prodromal Parkinson's Disease Speech

Michal Novotny(✉) and Jan Rusz

Czech Technical University in Prague, Technická 2, 166 27 Prague 6, Czech Republic
novotm26@fel.cvut.cz

Abstract. Speech, as one of the most complex human functions, involves over a hundred muscles and multiple brain areas, making it a valuable marker sensitive to neurodegenerative changes. With the advent of modern technologies, the link between speech disruption and neurodegeneration is gaining increasing research attention. The inexpensive and noninvasive nature of speech assessment, coupled with the broad availability of devices like smartphones, enables detailed speech monitoring during routine examinations or even in patients' daily lives. However, current knowledge of speech impairment largely relies on cross-sectional studies, lacking insights into individual speech changes associated with disease progression. Most studies have been conducted on clinically diagnosed PD cohorts, and the disease's heterogeneity, along with potentially non-linear speech deterioration, may limit the findings' applicability to the prodromal stage. To effectively study PD in its prodromal phase, large-scale, population-based prospective studies are necessary. However, with PD's 2% lifetime prevalence, designing and conducting such studies is challenging. To limit the study's scope, one approach is to preselect participants at higher risk for developing the disease, thereby reducing the study to a smaller, high-risk cohort of participants with known disease markers. Over the past decade, studies on automatic speech analysis in RBD patients enabled the direct characterization of speech patterns indicative of prodromal PD. This review synthesizes current research on automated speech analysis in individuals with RBD, exploring its potential as an early biomarker for neurodegenerative disease progression. We systematically reviewed studies published between 2014 and 2024, focusing on methodologies employing computational acoustic analysis.

Keywords: Prodromal Parkinson's Disease · REM Sleep Behavior Disorder · Speech

1 Introduction

Speech, as one of the most complex human functions, involves over a hundred muscles and multiple cortical and subcortical brain areas, making it a valuable marker sensitive to neurodegenerative changes [1]. Speech manifestations vary depending on the type, location, and severity of neurological damage. In Parkinson's disease (PD), speech is

J. I. Godino Llorente (Ed.): AAPS 2024, CCIS 2646, pp. 83–90, 2026.
https://doi.org/10.1007/978-3-032-07083-8_6

affected by common pathological manifestations such as bradykinesia and rigidity, leading to a characteristic alteration termed hypokinetic dysarthria [2]. Dysarthria has been identified as an early and prevalent sign of PD [3]. Given the importance of speech in social interactions, the gradual progression of speech impairment in late-stage PD significantly impacts patients' quality of life [4]. Moreover, the response of speech to available treatments is variable; while pharmacological treatments in early stages may improve some aspects of dysarthria, higher doses of medication or surgical treatments can induce new speech manifestations, such as stuttering or dyskinetic fluctuations [5].

With the advent of modern technologies, the link between speech disruption and neurodegeneration is gaining increasing research attention. The inexpensive and non-invasive nature of speech assessment, coupled with the broad availability of devices like smartphones, enables detailed speech monitoring during routine examinations or even in patients' daily lives [6, 7]. The complexity of speech and the early onset of speech manifestations make it a promising early biomarker for disease diagnosis and progression, with potential applications in future neuroprotective trials [8]. However, current knowledge of speech impairment largely relies on cross-sectional studies, lacking insights into individual speech changes associated with disease progression [9, 10]. Most studies have been conducted on clinically diagnosed PD cohorts, and the disease's heterogeneity, along with potentially non-linear speech deterioration, may limit the findings' applicability to the prodromal stage [1]. Additionally, the lack of large prospective studies focused on speech in PD leaves a knowledge gap regarding the earliest signs of speech-related disease onset [11].

To effectively study PD in its prodromal phase, large-scale, population-based prospective studies are essential [11]. However, with a lifetime prevalence of PD at 2%, designing and conducting such studies is challenging [12]. One approach to narrowing study scope is to preselect participants at higher risk of developing the disease, thereby focusing on a smaller, high-risk cohort with known disease markers. Recent studies have made significant progress in understanding prodromal PD by focusing on these high-risk cohorts. For instance, rapid eye movement sleep behavior disorder (RBD) is a strong risk factor for PD, with a high rate of conversion to the disease; approximately 3–4% of RBD patients develop PD each year, with 30–40% progressing within ten years [13]. Consequently, RBD cohorts provide an unprecedented opportunity to study PD in its prodromal phase [11].

In this review, we first summarize the current understanding of mechanisms underlying speech impairment across different stages of PD and discuss implications for identifying participants in the prodromal stage. We then review the state-of-the-art in prodromal PD speech assessment, with a focus on RBD high-risk cohorts. Finally, we highlight existing knowledge gaps and propose future research directions that may lead to new discoveries.

2 Prodromal Parkinson's Disease

For over two decades, Parkinson's disease has been recognized as a gradually progressing condition with a definable prodromal phase, affecting multiple domains including motor skills, cognition, and emotional state [11]. According to the Braak staging model,

PD may begin up to twenty years before clinical diagnosis, initially presenting with non-specific symptoms such as constipation, depression, impaired sense of smell, and sleep disturbances [14]. PD is now understood as a multisystem neurodegenerative disorder, with the Substantia Nigra affected relatively late in its course [14]. Recent research has also underscored the significant heterogeneity within PD, posing challenges to the development of effective neuroprotective therapies.

2.1 Braak Staging System

The Braak staging model, published two decades ago, progressively refined the understanding that Parkinson's disease (PD) is not merely a dopaminergic disorder but a multisystem neurodegeneration. According to this model, PD pathology begins in the lower brainstem and olfactory system, spreads toward the Substantia Nigra—where it damages nigrostriatal dopaminergic neurons—and eventually affects the neocortex in the later stages of the disease [14]. The staging is defined by the presence of Lewy bodies, aggregates of α-synuclein that cause cellular damage across various brain regions, with six distinct stages identified. The nigrostriatal system remains largely intact until stage 3, at which point hallmark motor symptoms, including bradykinesia, hypokinesia, akinesia, and rigidity, emerge. Therefore, the first and second stages are considered prodromal, with only subtle and nonspecific symptoms appearing.

While it is unlikely that speech is affected in the first Braak stage, we cannot entirely rule out the possibility of subtle speech impairments due to limited data from this earliest stage [1]. However, evidence from the second Braak stage reveals early speech impairment preceding damage to the nigrostriatal system, suggesting that monopitch and imprecise vowel articulation may originate from different brain regions.

During the third Braak stage, gradual damage to the nigrostriatal system results in the loss of approximately 80% of dopaminergic neurons, after which the hallmark symptoms appear, and the disease is typically diagnosed. Akinesia due to Substantia Nigra degradation leads to further deterioration in speech prosody, articulation, and voice quality. In the fourth and later Braak stages, PD progresses along nondopaminergic pathways, affecting subcortical and cortical brain regions and causing cognitive impairment. At these stages, speech may show temporal disruptions, linking this aspect of the disease to cognitive processing difficulties [1].

2.2 Rapid Eye Movement Sleep Behavior Disorder

Over the last decade, prospective studies targeting prodromal PD have investigated a variety of risk factors, with particularly promising findings for impaired olfaction [15–17], Substantia Nigra hyperechogenicity [16], and REM sleep behavior disorder (RBD) [16–18]. RBD, a parasomnia characterized by the loss of muscle atonia during REM sleep and dream enactment that can lead to injury for the patient or their bed partner, has shown a strong association with α-synuclein aggregation. This aggregation can lead to α-synucleinopathies such as multiple system atrophy, dementia with Lewy bodies, and PD, with PD being the most common phenoconversion.

Evidence confirms RBD as a significant risk factor for PD, with a high conversion rate to the disease. Approximately 6.3% of individuals with RBD develop PD each year, with 60.2% developing it within ten years and up to 73.5% within twelve years [19, 20]. In some cases, RBD has been observed as early as 25 years before a PD diagnosis, and three independent studies estimate RBD's prevalence in the general population at around 1% [21, 22]. Consequently, RBD cohorts provide an exceptional opportunity to study the prodromal phase of PD.

2.3 Other High-Risk Groups

Other high-risk groups for PD include carriers of genetic mutations; however, fully penetrant PD genes are rare, and common variants are generally too weak to be considered high-risk factors. Thus, only two gene mutations—glucocerebrosidase (GBA) and leucine-rich repeat kinase 2 (LRRK-2)—are both common enough and have sufficiently high penetrance to create viable cohorts. However, these subgroups are relatively uncommon in early PD, whereas RBD is present in approximately half of PD patients [11]. Consequently, most current research has focused on high-risk RBD cohorts, while GBA and LRRK-2 cohorts are primarily assembled for developing targeted therapies [11].

3 Speech in Prodromal Parkinson's Disease

In 2012, Postuma et al. published a study based on the UPDRS evaluation of 78 RBD participants, 20 of whom went on to develop PD. Among various markers, orofacial manifestations were identified as some of the earliest signs, appearing up to 10 years before diagnosis [3]. Since then, automated speech assessments in RBD populations have begun to characterize speech patterns in prodromal disease stages.

3.1 Acoustic Assessment of Motor Function

The first pilot study offering insight into RBD-related speech changes was published in 2016, examining speech in 16 RBD participants and 16 healthy, sex- and age-matched counterparts [22]. This study analyzed 15 markers capturing phonation, articulation, and prosody, and despite a limited sample size, confirmed disruptions in alternating motion rates and vowel articulation decay as early as the second Braak stage [22]. Additionally, findings indicated that these speech disruptions correlated with the severity of other motor symptoms. A subsequent study of connected speech among 50 RBD participants, 30 drug-naïve PD patients, and 50 healthy controls (HC) corroborated distorted articulation and altered speech timing [23]. In a blinded experiment, splitting the RBD group into subgroups with and without motor symptoms further verified a link between speech impairment and overall motor performance [23]. Jenacolas et al. later supported these findings, observing disrupted prosody, increased pause duration, and irregular rhythm in RBD speech [24].

To date, the largest study on automatic speech assessment in RBD included 448 participants (150 RBD, 149 PD, and 149 HC) across five languages—Czech, English, French, German, and Italian—with a 12-month follow-up [8]. This study aimed to identify speech biomarkers and assess potential language dependencies. Despite differences across languages, general patterns remained consistent, suggesting a shared pathomechanism. The most affected markers were monopitch, prolonged pauses, and imprecise consonants [8]. The study found no correlation between dysarthria and general motor performance, proposing that nondopaminergic brain circuits may play a role. Notably, while not statistically significant, the classification experiment identified harsh voice and slower speech rate as consistent features more frequent in RBD than PD. Harsh voice was identified as the strongest contributor to dysarthria progression [8]. The authors proposed that this distinction may reflect a different disease phenotype or that the dopaminergic medication potentially mitigates dysarthric symptoms in PD cohort [8].

In subsequent research Simek et al. demonstrated that cepstral peak prominence, reflecting voice breathiness over roughness, can distinguish early-stage PD, but not RBD, suggesting roughness is more characteristic of RBD, potentially indicating a distinct disease phenotype [25]. While the other studies support potential effect of dopaminergic treatment: Tykalova et al. found that short-term levodopa withdrawal in early-stage PD had no impact on speech while the long-term effect lead to dysarthria alleviation [26]. Furthermore, Rusz et al., using dopamine transporter single-photon emission computed tomography (DAT-SPECT), split RBD participants into those with normal and impaired olfaction. Participants with impaired olfaction but intact DAT-SPECT already showed monopitch, but follow-up revealed accelerated speech deterioration only in those with abnormal DAT-SPECT, suggesting faster dysarthria progression in these cases [27]. Similarly, a study on vowel articulation in RBD and de novo drug-naïve PD found that articulatory undershoot was more pronounced in those with hyposmia [28].

Alongside biomarker research, studies have explored the feasibility of smartphone-based analyses. Research on smartphone applicability began in 2018, revealing that voice disruption was among the most discriminating features of RBD [29]. Subsequent studies demonstrated that smartphones could reliably capture dysprosody, abnormal pause intervals, and slower speech timing [30]. Although promising, these recordings were conducted in lab settings. The first "in-the-wild" study by Arora et al. encouraged participants to take smartphones home and record four daily samples for a week [6]. This study extracted 327 speech features, achieving around 60% accuracy, highlighting the potential for clinical use as a prodromal biomarker. In 2024, Illner et al. analyzed real-world smartphone recordings from natural phone calls and short reading passages [7]. This study established the minimum phone call duration (20 s) and an optimal overall length of acquired data (18 min). Combining call and reading data yielded an area under the curve of 0.79 for distinguishing RBD from HC, outperforming lab settings (AUC 0.66). Notably, dysprosody was not evident in phone calls, and articulatory decay was less pronounced in reading tasks, possibly due to compensatory mechanisms [7].

3.2 Automatic Speech Recognition Based Cognitive Evaluation

With the development of automatic speech recognizers robust enough to reliably analyze dysarthric speech, it is now possible to examine morphological, semantic, and syntactic aspects of speech to assess cognitive functioning. In a study involving 40 RBD participants without mild cognitive impairment (MCI), 14 with MCI, as well as 40 PD participants without MCI and 15 with MCI, researchers found reduced content density in freely spoken monologues among RBD participants, regardless of MCI status. Individuals with MCI demonstrated lower lexical richness during storytelling tasks [31]. These findings suggest the presence of mild cognitive decline even at the prodromal disease stage.

Additionally, a study of 180 participants across seven sites and five languages indicated that cognitive decline could serve as a predictor of phenoconversion to neurodegeneration, with varying hazard ratios depending on conversion type: dementia-first, parkinsonism-first with MCI, or parkinsonism-first [32].

4 Current Gaps and Further Directions

Although speech assessments in RBD cohorts have significantly enhanced our understanding of the underlying dysarthria mechanisms in prodromal PD, several shortcomings must be acknowledged. First, while some studies have included follow-up examinations, all existing research is cross-sectional, highlighting the need for longitudinal studies that examine the development of specific dysarthria aspects. Second, despite RBD being the greatest known risk factor for PD development, only approximately 50% of PD patients exhibit RBD, indicating potential variability in dysarthria manifestations across different disease phenotypes. However, the widespread availability of smartphone technology and the sensitivity of automated speech assessments may facilitate large-scale prospective studies, yielding results with substantial generalizability.

Funding. This study was supported by the National Institute for Neurological Research (Programme EXCELES, ID Project No. LX22NPO5107 - Funded by the European Union – NextGeneration EUs.

References

1. Rusz, J., Krack, P., Tripoliti, E.: From Prodromal stages to clinical trials: the promise of digital speech biomarkers in Parkinson's disease. Neurosci. Biobehav. Rev. 105922 (2024)
2. Ho, A.K., Iansek, R., Marigliani, C., Bradshaw, J.L., Gates, S.: Speech impairment in a large sample of patients with Parkinson's disease. Behav. Neurol. **11**(3), 131–137 (1999)
3. Postuma, R.B., Lang, A.E., Gagnon, J.F., Pelletier, A., Montplaisir, J.Y.: How does parkinsonism start? Prodromal parkinsonism motor changes in idiopathic REM sleep behaviour disorder. Brain **135**(6), 1860–1870 (2012)
4. Finnimore, A., Theodoros, D., Rumbach, A.: The impact of PD Check-in, a model for supported self-managed maintenance of speech on the quality of life of people with parkinson's disease: a phase 1 study. Brain Sci. **12**(4), 433 (2022)
5. Tripoliti, E., et al.: Predictive factors of speech intelligibility following subthalamic nucleus stimulation in consecutive patients with Parkinson's disease. Mov. Disord. **29**(4), 532–538 (2014)
6. Arora, S., Lo, C., Hu, M., Tsanas, A.: Smartphone speech testing for symptom assessment in rapid eye movement sleep behavior disorder and Parkinson's disease. IEEE Access **9**, 44813–44824 (2021)
7. Illner, V. et al.: Smartphone voice calls provide early biomarkers of parkinsonism in rapid eye movement sleep behavior disorder. Mov. Disord. (2024)

8. Rusz, J., et al.: Speech biomarkers in rapid eye movement sleep behavior disorder and Parkinson disease. Ann. Neurol. **90**(1), 62–75 (2021)
9. Moro-Velazquez, L., Gomez-Garcia, J.A., Arias-Londoño, J.D., Dehak, N., Godino-Llorente, J.I.: Advances in Parkinson's disease detection and assessment using voice and speech: a review of the articulatory and phonatory aspects. Biomed. Signal Process. Control **66**, 102418 (2021)
10. Ngo, Q.C., Motin, M.A., Pah, N.D., Drotár, P., Kempster, P., Kumar, D.: Computerized analysis of speech and voice for Parkinson's disease: a systematic review. Comput. Methods Programs Biomed. **226**, 107133 (2022)
11. Postuma, R.B., Berg, D.: Prodromal Parkinson's disease: the decade past, the decade to come. Mov. Disord. **34**(5), 665–675 (2019)
12. Pringsheim, T., Jette, N., Frolkis, A., Steeves, T.D.: The prevalence of Parkinson's disease: a systematic review and meta-analysis. Mov. Disord. **29**(13), 1583–1590 (2014)
13. Zhang, H., et al.: Risk factors for phenoconversion in rapid eye movement sleep behavior disorder. Ann. Neurol. **91**(3), 404–416 (2022)
14. Braak, H., et al.: Staging of brain pathology related to sporadic Parkinson's disease. Neurobiol. Aging **24**(2), 197–211 (2003)
15. Berg, D., et al.: The PRIPS study: screening battery for subjects at risk for Parkinson's disease. Eur. J. Neurol. **20**(1), 102–108 (2013)
16. Berg, D., et al.: Enlarged hyperechogenic substantia nigra as a risk marker for Parkinson's disease. Mov. Disord. **28**(2), 216–219 (2013)
17. Jennings, D., et al. and PARS investigators: conversion to Parkinson disease in the pars hyposmic and dopamine transporter–deficit prodromal cohort. JAMA Neurol. **74**(8), 933–940 (2017)
18. Gaenslen, A., et al.: Prodromal features for Parkinson's disease–baseline data from the TREND study. Eur. J. Neurol. **21**(5), 766–772 (2014)
19. Postuma, R.B., et al.: Risk and predictors of dementia and parkinsonism in idiopathic REM sleep behaviour disorder: a multicentre study. Brain **142**(3), 744–759 (2019)
20. Claassen, D.O., Josephs, K.A., Ahlskog, J.E., Silber, M.H., Tippmann-Peikert, M., Boeve, B.F.: REM sleep behavior disorder preceding other aspects of synucleinopathies by up to half a century. Neurology **75**(6), 494–499 (2010)
21. Kang, S.H., Yoon, I.Y., Lee, S.D., Han, J.W., Kim, T.H., Kim, K.W.: REM sleep behavior disorder in the Korean elderly population: prevalence and clinical characteristics. Sleep **36**(8), 1147–1152 (2013)
22. Rusz, J., et al.: Quantitative assessment of motor speech abnormalities in idiopathic rapid eye movement sleep behaviour disorder. Sleep Med. **19**, 141–147 (2014)
23. Hlavnička, J., Čmejla, R., Tykalová, T., Šonka, K., Růžička, E., Rusz, J.: Automated analysis of connected speech reveals early biomarkers of Parkinson's disease in patients with rapid eye movement sleep behaviour disorder. Sci. Rep. **7**(1), 12 (2017)
24. Jeancolas, L., et al.: Voice characteristics from isolated rapid eye movement sleep behavior disorder to early Parkinson's disease. Parkinsonism Relat. Disord. **95**, 86–91 (2022)
25. Šimek, M., Rusz, J.: Validation of cepstral peak prominence in assessing early voice changes of Parkinson's disease: effect of speaking task and ambient noise. J. Acoust. Soc. Am. **150**(6), 4522–4533 (2021)
26. Tykalova, T., Novotny, M., Ruzicka, E., Dusek, P., Rusz, J.: Short-term effect of dopaminergic medication on speech in early-stage Parkinson's disease. npj Parkinson's Dis. **8**(1), 22 (2022)
27. Rusz, J., et al.: Dysprosody in isolated REM sleep behavior disorder with impaired olfaction but intact nigrostriatal pathway. Mov. Disord. **37**(3), 619–623 (2022)
28. Skrabal, D., et al.: Articulatory undershoot of vowels in isolated REM sleep behavior disorder and early Parkinson's disease. npj Parkinson's Dis. **8**(1), 137 (2022)

29. Arora, S., et al.: Smartphone motor testing to distinguish idiopathic REM sleep behavior disorder, controls, and PD. Neurology **91**(16), e1528–e1538 (2018)
30. Rusz, J., et al.: Smartphone allows capture of speech abnormalities associated with high risk of developing Parkinson's disease. IEEE Trans. Neural Syst. Rehabil. Eng. **26**(8), 1495–1507 (2018)
31. Šubert, M., et al.: Linguistic abnormalities in isolated rapid eye movement sleep behavior disorder. Mov. Disord. **37**(9), 1872–1882 (2022)
32. Šubert, M., et al.: Spoken Language alterations can predict phenoconversion in isolated rapid eye movement sleep behavior disorder: a multicenter study. Ann. Neurol. **95**(3), 530–543 (2024)

Reverberation Time as an Acoustic Biomarker for Speech Impairment in Parkinson Disease

Fasih Haider[1(✉)], Nina Diviza[1], David P. Breen[1,2,3], Angela Christine Roberts[4,5,6], and Saturnino Luz[1]

[1] Usher Institute, University of Edinburgh, Edinburgh, UK
{fhaider,nina.diviza,david.breen,s.luz}@ed.ac.uk
[2] Centre for Clinical Brain Sciences, University of Edinburgh, Edinburgh, UK
[3] Anne Rowling Regenerative Neurology Clinic, Institute for Neuroscience and Cardiovascular Research, University of Edinburgh, Edinburgh, UK
[4] School of Communication Sciences and Disorders, Western University, London, ON, Canada
angela.roberts@uwo.ca
[5] Department of Computer Sciences, Western University, London, ON, Canada
[6] Canadian Centre for Activity and Aging, Western University, London, ON, Canada

Abstract. Parkinson disease (PD) is a neurodegenerative disease that can impair speech production. In PD, speech impairments are typically characterised by reduced vocal loudness, monotone speech, and distorted articulation. We hypothesise that speech impairment in PD could alter energy decay patterns in speech, leading to changes in reverberation time for 60 dB of decay in sound pressure (RT60). To determine whether the reverberation characteristics can help to differentiate between healthy and PD-affected speech, RT60 was derived from speech segments extracted from recordings in Castilian Spanish and English using the Schroeder's Integration algorithm. A t-test analysis revealed significant differences between the PD group and healthy controls in both languages. In addition, classification tasks were performed based on the descriptive statistics and temporal features of RT60 for each participant, using logistic regression, decision tree and random forest classifiers. The random forest classifier provided the best accuracy (0.77) on the Castilian Spanish data and was tested on the English data, yielding an accuracy of 0.67. This study demonstrates that RT60 can be effectively repurposed for PD detection.

Keywords: Parkinson disease · reverberation time · digital biomarkers

1 Introduction

Parkinson disease (PD) is the second most common neurodegenerative disease after Alzheimer's disease with its prevalence projected to double to 12 million by 2040 [2]. Early detection of PD is crucial for delivering effective treatment, managing symptoms, enhancing quality of life, and supporting the development and assessment of therapies that aim to slow or alter disease progression. To this

J. I. Godino Llorente (Ed.): AAPS 2024, CCIS 2646, pp. 91–102, 2026.
https://doi.org/10.1007/978-3-032-07083-8_7

day, the set of criteria established by the International Parkinson and Movement Disorder Society (MDS) in 2015 [17] remains essential for diagnosing clinical PD [24]. The MDS criteria represents a revised version of the Queen's Square Brain Bank Criteria [10, 17], and expands on it by providing exclusionary conditions. According to the MDS criteria, a thorough neurological examination is required to verify the presence of bradykinesia in combination with muscle rigidity and/or tremor at rest. For a clinical PD diagnosis to be confirmed, clinicians use defined features to rule out other non-PD causes of parkinsonism. The diagnosis can be made at one of two levels of certainty: "clinically established", which prioritises specificity at the expense of sensitivity, and "clinically probable PD", which emphasises sensitivity. Although these well-established criteria have demonstrated high sensitivity (96%) and specificity (95%) for clinically probable PD [18], the specificity (87%) for clinically probable PD in patients with a disease duration of less than 5 years is notably reduced, as reported by Tolosa et al. in their review paper [24]. Since PD diagnosis relies on a clinician, developing tools to facilitate remote screening would be of significant value. To address this problem, machine learning and speech processing methods have been utilised to discover non-invasive and cost-effective clinical markers derived from speech.

PD can significantly affect speech production, with hypokinetic dysarthria observed in 70%–90% of individuals with PD [20]. Hypokinetic dysarthria in PD often manifests as reduced vocal loudness, weakened vocal strength, monopitch production, imprecise articulation of consonants, longer pauses at non-grammatical boundaries, and short rushes of speech [22]. Impairments in voice quality tend to emerge early in PD [6, 11], while changes in articulation and speech fluency typically develop at later stages [22].

Numerous diagnostic speech markers have been proposed in the literature. Moro-Velázquez et al. [14] conducted a review of speech features and machine learning methods for automatic PD detection and severity assessment. The review included studies published between 1956–2020, and were grouped into: phonatory, articulatory, prosodic, and cognitive-linguistic. Another review conducted by Ngo et al. [15] covering 2010–2021, analysed 189 studies to identify the most suitable computerised methods for the automatic detection of PD. A more recent survey of the literature [1] concluded that jitter, shimmer, harmonic-to-noise ratio, fundamental frequency, and Mel Frequency Cepstral Coefficients were the most investigated features among the included 102 studies and 5 reviews.

These studies also highlight the need for interpretable features that clinicians can easily integrate into clinical practice [15, 19], and the necessity to explore features beyond phonatory and articulatory ones [14]. There is also a demand for features that are not language- or context-specific and translate well to new recording environments and cohorts [1, 14, 15, 19]. Therefore, considerable effort has been directed towards extracting speech features from multi-lingual data. In one such study, the most discriminative and robust (i.e., showing similar behaviour across languages) acoustic and cognitive features for distinguishing between PD and healthy control (HC) groups across 6 languages were fundamental frequency standard deviation, speech rhythm standard deviation, pause percentage, pause duration, silence duration, and linguistic features such as length of narrative, number of nouns, and auxiliary verbs produced [3]. Using the same datasets, deep embeddings (such as wav2vec 2.0) outperformed interpretable features (grouped into prosodic, linguistic, and cognitive features), with a reported F1-score of 88% and 79% in multi-lingual and cross-lingual experiments, respectively [4]. A different study [9] examined 33 acoustic features extracted from speech recorded during a short text reading task, sustained vowel phonation [a], and a diadochokinetic task (DDK) of repeated syllables [pa]-[ta]-[ka]. The participants were native speakers of Czech, American English, Hebrew, Colombian Spanish, and Italian. The best language-agnostic predictors identified, in terms of global normalised combination of importance coefficients and Shapley values, were second formant prominence, monopitch, and pause frequency during text reading. The XGBoost classifier achieved an accuracy between 67–85%, depending on the language, with the classifier demonstrating an accuracy of 75% for all languages combined.

Considering the range of speech tasks and equipment required to gather speech data, it may be preferable to identify speech markers from data that can be recorded remotely, regardless of acoustic environment, and that could be used for remote PD assessment and monitoring. In this study, we propose using RT60, derived from speech recordings of PD and HC participants in English and Castilian Spanish, to investigate whether reverberation characteristics can serve as reliable biomarkers for differentiating between healthy and PD-affected speech. RT60 measures the time it takes for sound to decay by 60 decibels after the sound source stops. In PD, speech impairments are typically characterised by reduced vocal loudness, monotone speech, and distorted articulation.

Although RT60 is traditionally used to assess room acoustics, in this paper we investigate whether its application to speech recordings may offer new opportunities for detecting speech deterioration in PD. We hypothesise that speech impairment in PD could alter energy decay patterns in speech, leading to changes in RT60. We employ Schroeder integration [23], a method that computes the cumulative energy decay of a signal, to estimate the decay time of the speech signal itself, focusing on speech dynamics of PD vs. HC. This study addresses the following research question: Can reverberation time (RT60), derived from natural speech recordings, serve as a reliable acoustic marker for neuromotor degradation in PD? We hypothesize that reduced RT60 values in PD speech reflect more rapid energy decay, caused by impaired subglottal pressure and insufficient articulatory effort. The contributions of this work are:

1. a novel application of RT60 estimation using Schroeder's integral for speech analysis in PD, and
2. an empirical evaluation showing that RT60 estimated by Schroeder's integral can reveal measurable differences between PD and HC speech, offering potential as an acoustic biomarker for PD.

2 Method and Analysis

This study was conducted using two distinct datasets, which served as the primary sources of speech data for all analyses - Mobile Device Voice Recordings at King's College London (MDVR-KCL) [8] and the Castilian Spanish corpus of Parkinsonian speech (NeuroVoz) [12,13].

MDVR-KCL: This dataset contains speech samples in English from 37 native and non-native speakers (16 with PD, 21 HC) collected via a mobile device at King's College London in September 2017. Participants had both early and advanced stages of PD.

The examination room had an area of 10 square meters and a reverberation time of approximately 500 ms. Participants were recorded speaking using a Motorola Moto G4 Smartphone, with a 44.1 kHz sampling rate and a bit depth of 16 Bit (audio CD quality) via the "Toggle Recording App" functionality developed by the authors from [8]. This functionality was deployed as a standalone android application allowing the voice capturing service to run in the background, starting and stopping the recording via the on/off hook signals of the smartphone. As an initial step in the data collection process, participants were instructed to relax in a quiet environment and subsequently initiate a telephone call to one of the researchers. Then they were asked to read one of the two paragraphs of text ("The North Wind and the Sun", "Tech. Engin. Computer applications in geography snippet"), depending on the participant's preference. Following the reading task, realistic and spontaneous telephone conversations were recorded for each participant. During this portion of the recording session, participants were encouraged to engage in natural dialogue by speaking about a range of familiar and personally relevant topics, such as their favourite places to visit, personal hobbies and interests, or traffic conditions. This conversational approach was designed to elicit authentic speech patterns reflective of everyday communication. The recording session concluded with a natural farewell exchange, signalling the end of the call.

The metadata contains annotated clinical information about participants including health status label, Hoehn & Yahr (H-Y) [7] stage, expert peer-reviewed Unified Parkinson's Disease Rating Scale (UPDRS) [16] scores using part II question 5 (Activities of Daily Living - Speech), and expert assessed scores using UPDRS part III question 18 (Motor Examination - Speech). All HC participants were assessed using the same UPDRS questions for comparison, since voice degradation correlates with PD but does not fully overlap [8]. Therefore, the dataset includes one HC participant (ID31) with UPDRS II-5 and III-18 scores of 1, and some PD patients with scores of 0, reflecting the expert's inability to detect voice degradation and not ambiguity in the data. Gender, age, and occupation information were not recorded.

NeuroVoz: This dataset contains speech samples from 112 native speakers of Castilian Spanish (46 females, 61 males, and one participant without gender information), evenly distributed by health status (58 HC, 54 people with

PD), and by age (PD group's average age of 71.13 ± 10.62 years, and 64.04 ± 10.26 years for the HC group). To be included in the PD group, participants had to be diagnosed with PD by the Neurology Services of Hospital General Universitario Gregorio Marañón and Hospital Universitario de Fuenlabrada, Madrid, Spain, without applying any restrictions regarding the onset time of their clinical signals. HC volunteers had no neurological conditions, no PD diagnosis, and were not professional voice users. They were asked to complete a neurological survey and selected to match the age and sex distribution of the PD group.

The data collected amounts to 2,977 audio recordings with 26.88 ± 3.35 recordings on average per participant. All participants were recorded in the same acoustic environment using a AKG® C420 headset microphone. PD patients were recorded in an ON state having taken their prescribed medication, where applicable, 2–5 h before the session.

Speech was elicited using a wide variety of tasks: sustained vowel phonation of five Spanish vowels, DDK tasks, 16 listen-and-repeat sentences, and spontaneous monologues elicited through picture description. The speech collected through listen-and-repeat tasks and spontaneous monologues were annotated by expert transcribers to capture any deviations from the script and mispronunciations.

Demographic information about participants contains age, sex, and employment status. Clinical data include the number of years since diagnosis, and the presence of specific symptoms (vocal tremor, mandibular tremor, cephalic tremor, sialorrhea, dysphagia, and hypophonic voice) was recorded as a dichotomous variable. Medication details were collected in a free text field, along with UPDRS score and H-Y stage. In addition, participants were assessed using Grade, Roughness, Breathiness, Asthenia, and Strain (GRBAS) perceptual scale [5].

2.1 Inclusion Criteria

In the present study, our analysis focused on spontaneous speech, specifically on the spontaneous monologues elicited through the picture description task from the NeuroVoz dataset and the phone conversations from the MDVR-KCL dataset. To ensure the integrity and quality of the analysis, every individual recording underwent a meticulous manual inspection using high-quality professional headphones. This inspection process involved identifying and excluding any segments that were affected by background noise, overlapping speech, or other forms of signal distortion.

In the case of the MDVR-KCL dataset, all audio segments containing overlapping talk were systematically removed. Following this cleaning process, the final dataset consisted of 15 participants diagnosed with PD, contributing a total of 104 audio files, which together account for approximately 17 min of usable speech. Additionally, 21 HC participants remained in the dataset, with 162 audio files amounting to approximately 22 min of speech.

In contrast, for the NeuroVoz dataset, no recordings or segments were excluded during pre-processing. As a result, this dataset provided roughly 12 min of speech from 23 individuals with PD, and about 39 min of speech from 51 HC participants.

This rigorous selection and pre-processing process ensured that only high-quality, non-overlapping, and noise-free speech data were retained for subsequent analysis.

2.2 Speech Segmentation and Pre-processing

The pre-processing stage of the audio data involved a structured sequence of signal processing operations, implemented using the `pydub` library in Python [21]. These steps were carefully designed to prepare the recordings for subsequent analysis by removing the silent segments from the utterance and ensuring consistency of the amplitude levels in all speech segments.

The process began with peak normalisation, a technique aimed at standardising the amplitude levels across audio files. In this step, the maximum amplitude level was identified within each recording and remaining portions of the signal were adjusted proportionally to that level. This step ensures that all audio files have comparable loudness levels, which is crucial for reliable feature extraction.

Following normalisation, an energy-based Voice Activity Detection (VAD) algorithm was employed to isolate segments containing actual speech. This algorithm works by analysing the energy of the signal over time to distinguish between speech and non-speech regions. Only those segments that were longer than 1 s and quieter than a threshold of -40dB relative to the maximum amplitude of the whole audio file were identified as silence and dropped.

Finally, to maintain uniformity in the length of the extracted speech segments and to avoid overly long stretches of uninterrupted speech, a maximum duration limit of six seconds was imposed on each segment. Any speech portions exceeding this threshold were split accordingly.

Altogether, this comprehensive pre-processing pipeline ensured that the dataset contained high-quality, standardised speech segments suitable for robust and reliable analysis. A flowchart outlining the pre-processing pipeline is presented in Fig. 1.

Overall, the analysis was conducted on speech samples from 36 participants from the MDVR-KCL dataset (comprising 15 individuals diagnosed with PD and 21 HC), as well as 74 participants from the NeuroVoz dataset (comprising 23 individuals with PD and 51 HC).

Within the MDVR-KCL dataset, the average number of extracted speech segments per participant was calculated to be 15.33 for the HC group, with a standard deviation (SD) of 4.79. For the PD group in the same dataset, participants contributed an average of 16.4 segments, with a standard deviation of 6.88. In terms of total speech duration, each participant in the HC group contributed an average of 61.12 s of usable speech data (SD = 22.6 s), while participants in the PD group provided an average of 58.51 s (SD = 31.57 s).

For the NeuroVoz dataset, the healthy control group exhibited an average of 9.39 speech segments per participant, with a standard deviation of 4.16, whereas the PD group had a lower average of 6.96 segments, with a standard deviation of 3.32. Regarding speech duration, participants in the HC group contributed

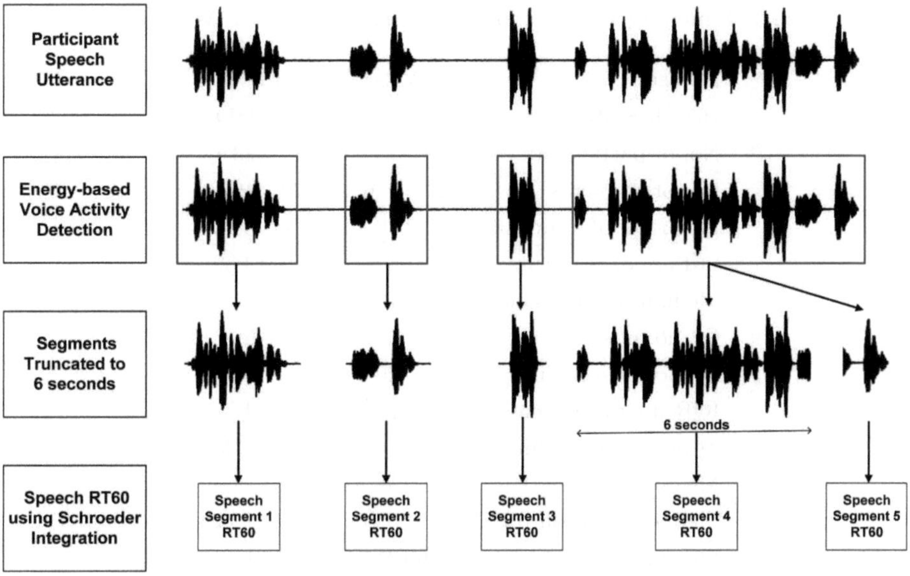

Fig. 1. Pre-processing pipeline in extracting speech segments to compute RT60 from participant speech utterances. The pipeline was implemented in Python using `pydub` [21]. After removing segments with noise or overlapping speech, peak normalisation was applied to each utterance. Then, speech segments were extracted using an energy-based voice activity detection algorithm. Segments that were longer than 1 s and quieter than a threshold of -40dB relative to the maximum amplitude of the whole audio file were dropped. The maximum duration of a speech segment was set to 6 s. Finally, RT60 was computed for each of the segments.

an average of 40.55 s of speech (SD = 19.14 s), while those in the PD group contributed significantly less, with an average of 24.39 s (SD = 10.11 s).

A comprehensive summary of the speech data analysed in this study, including the number of participants, segments, and speech durations for each group, is provided in Table 1.

2.3 RT60 Feature Extraction

Computing RT60 began with the calculation of the normalised energy decay curve $E(n)$ by applying Schroeder's integral, as shown in Equation (1), where N is the length of the input speech segment $x(i)$:

$$E(n) = \frac{\sum_{i=n}^{N-1} |x(i)|^2}{\sum_{i=0}^{N-1} |x(i)|^2} \tag{1}$$

RT60 was then estimated from the energy decay curve. The energy curve $E(n)$ is converted to decibels(i.e. $E_{\mathrm{dB}}(n) = 10 \cdot \log_{10}(E(n))$), and the algorithm identifies the time points at which the energy decay ($E_{\mathrm{dB}}(n)$) reaches –5 dB

Table 1. Summary statistics for MDVR-KCL and NeuroVoz datasets

Dataset	MDVR-KCL		NeuroVoz	
Health Status	**HC**	**PD**	**HC**	**PD**
No. of participants	21	15	51	23
No. of segments	322	246	479	160
Mean no. of segments	15.33	16.40	9.39	6.96
Std no. of segments	4.79	6.88	4.16	3.32
Median no. of segments	15	16	9	6
Q1 no. of segments	12	11.5	6	5
Q3 no. of segments	19	20	13	9
IQR no. of segments	7	8.5	7	4
Total duration (min)	21.39	14.63	34.46	9.35
Mean duration (s)	61.12	58.51	40.55	24.39
Median duration (s)	61.54	54.66	39.56	22.26
Std duration (s)	22.60	31.57	19.14	10.11

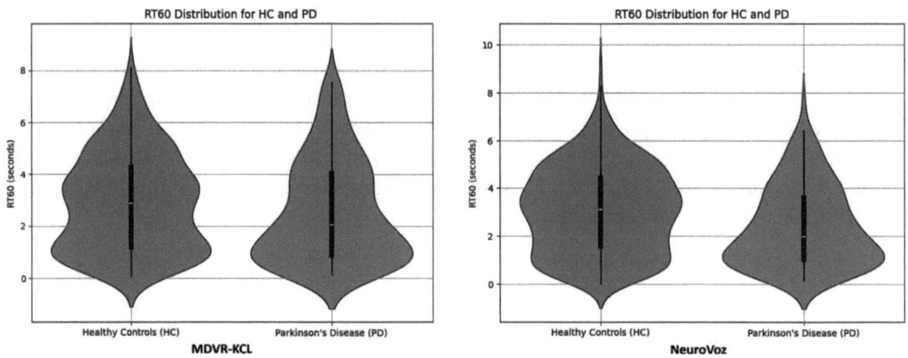

Fig. 2. RT 60 using Schroeder Integration (SI).

($n_{5\mathrm{dB}}$) and –35 dB ($n_{35\mathrm{dB}}$). Later, time is extrapolated from a 30 dB decay interval to a 60 dB decay interval (i.e. $RT60 = (n_{35\mathrm{dB}} - n_{5\mathrm{dB}}) \cdot \frac{60}{35-5}$), where $n_{35\mathrm{dB}}$ and $n_{5\mathrm{dB}}$ are the times at which the energy decay curve crosses –35 dB and –5 dB, respectively. This method provides an estimation of RT60 by leveraging the linearity of the energy decay in logarithmic space within the selected decay range.

2.4 Statistical Analysis

For each segment we calculated the RT60 and performed a t-test analysis. Table 2 and Fig. 2 demonstrate that PD speech exhibited distinct reverberation characteristics, with altered energy decay patterns compared to healthy speech. These differences suggest that RT60 could be a valuable acoustic feature for distinguishing PD speech from healthy speech.

Table 2. RT60 Comparison and Performance of Machine Learning Classifiers (MLC) on MDVR-KCL and NeuroVoz Datasets, Accuracy (A), Macro Accuracy (MA), Sensitivity (Sens.) and Specificity (Spec.)

Dataset	Group/MLC	RT60 Analysis				MLC Performance			
		mean (s)	SD	t-stat	p	A	MA	Sens.	Spec.
MDVR-KCL	PD	2.57	1.95	2.2434	0.025	–	–	–	–
	HC	2.94	1.86			–	–	–	–
	LR	–	–	–	–	0.67	0.66	0.60	0.71
	DT	–	–	–	–	0.69	0.66	0.47	0.86
	RF	–	–	–	–	**0.72**	**0.72**	0.73	0.72
NeuroVoz	PD	2.41	1.66	4.43	0.001	–	–	–	–
	HC	3.10	1.79			–	–	–	–
	LR	–	–	–	–	0.70	0.73	0.61	0.78
	DT	–	–	–	–	0.76	0.70	0.57	0.84
	RF	–	–	–	–	**0.77**	0.69	0.48	**0.90**
Cross Corpora (RF)		–	–	–	–	0.67	0.62	0.33	**0.90**

2.5 Machine Learning Methods

To explore this further using machine learning methods, we performed classification tasks (10-fold cross validation) using logistic regression (LR), decision tree (DT) and random forest (RF) classifiers. For each audio recording, we calculated descriptive statistical features (mean, standard deviation, minimum, first quartile, median, third quartile, the maximum RT60 values). Additionally, temporal features were computed (mean, standard deviation, minimum, and maximum of the first-order derivative of RT60 values).

3 Results

The results are summarised in Table 2. For each dataset, the mean RT60 is presented for the PD and HC groups, as well as the performance metrics for the machine learning classifiers employed. A t-test analysis revealed significant differences between the PD and HC groups in both datasets. For the MDVR-KCL dataset, RF provided the highest accuracy of 0.72 with a macro average of 0.72. For the NeuroVoz dataset, RF yielded the best accuracy of 0.77. We noticed that the RF classifier provided the best accuracy for the NeuroVoz data. Therefore, we trained a classifier using the NeuroVoz data and tested it on the MDVR-KCL data. This resulted in an accuracy of 0.67, demonstrating the usefulness of RT60 across different languages.

4 Discussion

Beyond the quantitative results, this study offers meaningful insights into energy decay dynamics as a lens for understanding speech degradation in PD, and the role that reverberation-based features can play in capturing these impairments. Reverberation time, as measured through RT60, reflects not only the acoustic environment but also the consistency and forcefulness of vocal energy produced by the speaker. In PD, reductions in subglottal pressure and weakened articulatory gestures are known to limit the clarity and sharpness of speech, resulting in rapid energy decay, which is reflected in the RT60 values.

Importantly, our results suggest that RT60 is sensitive to both phonatory and articulatory components of speech production. This sensitivity makes it a compelling candidate for characterising dysarthria severity in a non-invasive, language-independent way. The reduced RT60 values observed in PD participants were consistent across both datasets, indicating that the measure is robust to variability in task demands and content.

Furthermore, by leveraging RT60 as a single scalar descriptor of temporal energy decay, this work contributes to ongoing efforts to simplify the acoustic assessment of motor speech disorders. Unlike more complex spectral or prosodic features that require task-specific extraction and interpretation, RT60 provides a straightforward and interpretable signal property. It integrates information about respiratory drive, glottal function, and vocal tract dynamics, making it a holistic measure that captures multiple dimensions of motor speech control.

These findings also resonate with clinical observations, where patients with PD often present with "blurred" or "muffled" speech, impressions that may be acoustically rooted in delayed energy dissipation. As such, RT60 could complement perceptual assessments by offering a reproducible, quantitative proxy of these qualitative impressions. Moreover, it bridges the gap between speech science and clinical applicability, offering a practical route for embedding acoustic markers into digital health technologies for early diagnosis and monitoring of PD.

The RT60 time calculated using Schroeder Integration could be prone to artifacts, such as noise in the speech signal and room acoustics. Developing methods to estimate vocal cord reverberation time could be a focus of future work. Another limitation of this study is the small data size.

5 Conclusion

In conclusion, this study demonstrates that reverberation time, traditionally used for room acoustics, can be repurposed for PD detection. By estimating RT60 from speech recordings, we offer a new, objective measure for characterising vocal impairments in PD, which could be integrated into automated systems for early disease detection. In future work, we would like to explore how RT60 could be used to determine disease stage and to monitor PD progression.

Acknowledgments. This study was supported by the Medical Research Council (Precision Medicine Grant MR/W006804/1 to ND) and the Canada Research Chairs Program (grant number CRC-2022-00089 to AR), whose contributions are gratefully acknowledged. We would also like to express our sincere gratitude for the public availability of the MDVR-KCL and NeuroVoz datasets [8,12,13]. Access to these resources has been instrumental in supporting our research and contributing to advancements in the field.

Disclosure of Interests. The authors have no competing interests.

References

1. Amato, F., Saggio, G., Cesarini, V., Olmo, G., Costantini, G.: Machine learning- and statistical-based voice analysis of Parkinson's disease patients: a survey. Expert Syst. Appl. **219**, 119651 (2023)
2. Dorsey, E.R., Sherer, T., Okun, M.S., Bloem, B.R.: The emerging evidence of the parkinson pandemic. J. Parkinsons Dis. **8**(s1), S3–S8 (2018)
3. Favaro, A., Moro-Velázquez, L., Butala, A., Motley, C., Cao, T., Stevens, R.D., Villalba, J., Dehak, N.: Multilingual evaluation of interpretable biomarkers to represent language and speech patterns in Parkinson's disease. Front. Neurol. **14**, 1142642 (2023)
4. Favaro, A., et al.: Interpretable speech features vs. DNN embeddings: what to use in the automatic assessment of Parkinson's disease in multi-lingual scenarios. Comput. Biol. Med. **166**, 107559 (2023)
5. Hirano, M.: Clinical examination of voice. Dis. Hum. Commun. **5**, 1–99 (1981)
6. Ho, A.K., Iansek, R., Marigliani, C., Bradshaw, J.L., Gates, S.: Speech impairment in a large sample of patients with parkinson's disease. Behav. Neurol. **11**(3), 131–137 (1999)
7. Hoehn, M.M., Yahr, M.D.: Parkinsonism: onset, progression, and mortality. Neurology **17**(5), 427–427 (1967)
8. Jaeger, H., Trivedi, D., Stadtschnitzer, M.: Mobile device voice recordings at king's college london (mdvr-kcl) from both early and advanced parkinson's disease patients and healthy controls (2019). https://doi.org/10.5281/zenodo.2867216, https://doi.org/10.5281/zenodo.2867216
9. Kovac, D., et al.: Exploring digital speech biomarkers of hypokinetic dysarthria in a multilingual cohort. Biomed. Signal Process. Control **88**, 105667 (2024)
10. Lees, A.J., Hardy, J., Revesz, T.: Parkinson's disease. The Lancet **373**(9680), 2055–2066 (2009)
11. Ma, A., Lau, K.K., Thyagarajan, D.: Voice changes in parkinson's disease: what are they telling us? J. Clin. Neurosci. **72**, 1–7 (2020)
12. Mendes-Laureano, J., et al.: Neurovoz: a castillian spanish corpus of parkinsonian speech. arXiv:2403.02371 (2024)
13. Mendes-Laureano, J., et al.: NeuroVoz: a Castillian Spanish corpus of parkinsonian speech (1.0.0) [data set] (2024)
14. Moro-Velazquez, L., Gomez-Garcia, J.A., Arias-Londoño, J.D., Dehak, N., Godino-Llorente, J.I.: Advances in Parkinson's disease detection and assessment using voice and speech: a review of the articulatory and phonatory aspects. Biomed. Signal Process. Control **66**, 102418 (2021)

15. Ngo, Q.C., Motin, M.A., Pah, N.D., Drotár, P., Kempster, P., Kumar, D.: Computerized analysis of speech and voice for Parkinson's disease: a systematic review. Comput. Methods Programs Biomed. **226**, 107133 (2022)
16. on Rating Scales for Parkinson's Disease, M.D.S.T.F.: The unified parkinson's disease rating scale (updrs): status and recommendations. Movement Disorders **18**(7), 738–750 (2003)
17. Postuma, R.B., et al.: Mds clinical diagnostic criteria for parkinson's disease. Mov. Disord. **30**(12), 1591–1601 (2015)
18. Postuma, R.B., et al.: Validation of the mds clinical diagnostic criteria for parkinson's disease. Mov. Disord. **33**(10), 1601–1608 (2018)
19. Ramanarayanan, V., Lammert, A.C., Rowe, H.P., Quatieri, T.F., Green, J.R.: Speech as a biomarker: opportunities, interpretability, and challenges. Perspect. ASHA Special Interest Groups **7**(1), 276–283 (2022)
20. Ramig, L.O., Fox, C., Sapir, S.: Speech treatment for parkinson's disease. Expert Rev. Neurother. **8**(2), 297–309 (2008)
21. Robert, J.: Pydub. https://github.com/jiaaro/pydub (2011), MIT License
22. Rohl, A., Gutierrez, S., Johari, K., Greenlee, J., Tjaden, K., Roberts, A.: Speech dysfunction, cognition, and parkinson's disease. Prog. Brain Res. **269**(1), 153–173 (2022)
23. Schroeder, M.R.: New method of measuring reverberation time. J. Acoust. Soc. Am. **37**(6_Supplement), 1187–1188 (1965)
24. Tolosa, E., Garrido, A., Scholz, S.W., Poewe, W.: Challenges in the diagnosis of parkinson's disease. Lancet Neurol. **20**(5), 385–397 (2021)

On Detection of Depression in Parkinson's Disease Patients' Speech: Handcrafted Features vs. Speech Foundation Models

Tilak Purohit[1,2](✉), Barbara Ruvolo[1], Juan Rafael Orozco-Arroyave[3], and Mathew Magimai.-Doss[1]

[1] Idiap Research Institute, Martigny, Switzerland
{tilak.purohit,mathew.magimaidoss}@idiap.ch
[2] EPFL, École polytechnique fédérale de Lausanne, Lausanne, Switzerland
[3] GITA Lab, Universidad de Antioquia, Medellín, Colombia

Abstract. This study investigates speech-based depression detection in individuals with Parkinson's disease (PD), comparing two feature representation approaches: interpretable handcrafted acoustic features and non-interpretable representations derived from Speech Foundation Models (SFMs). Using the DAIC-WOZ corpus for typical depression (non-PD speech) and the PD-Depression corpus for depression in atypical speech (PD speech). We first examine the viability of handcrafted features and then analyse how acoustic descriptors differ across these conditions. We then evaluate SFM-based representations on the PD-Depression dataset using a cross-validation-based layer selection methodology. Results suggest that handcrafted features yield better classification performance for depression in PD speech compared to SFM embeddings. Analysis shows that while typical depression is marked by pitch instability and reduced vocal quality, speech from PD patients with depression exhibits broader spectral variability, likely due to motor impairments associated with hypokinetic dysarthria.

Keywords: Depression detection · Parkinson's disease · Interpretable features · Speech Foundation Models

1 Introduction

Depressive disorder is a common mental health condition that affects an estimated 5% of the global adult population, according to the World Health Organization [41]. It is associated with a range of emotional, cognitive, and behavioral symptoms [38], such as persistent low mood, anxiety, and slowed motor activity, and in some cases may lead to suicidal thoughts [1]. Diagnosis typically depends on clinical interviews, which can vary in consistency and may contribute to heterogeneous assessments [4,6,24]. This highlights the relevance of developing reliable automated approaches to support the screening of depression across its diverse manifestations.

J. I. Godino Llorente (Ed.): AAPS 2024, CCIS 2646, pp. 103–117, 2026.
https://doi.org/10.1007/978-3-032-07083-8_8

In the speech community, numerous studies have explored the use of acoustic features for detecting depression, demonstrating the potential of vocal indicators [7,15,27,28,39,43]. These studies typically involve statistical analysis of features such as fundamental frequency (F0), intensity, and various spectral properties, suggesting their relevance as possible markers for depression screening. In recent years, artificial neural network (ANN)-based methods have become increasingly popular for this task, showing promising results in capturing speech patterns linked to depressive states [9,19,26,42]. While these methods often outperform traditional handcrafted approaches in terms of accuracy, they generally lack interpretability and are constrained by the availability of sufficient labeled data for training.

Although the field has seen substantial advances, accurately detecting depression from speech remains difficult due to the diverse manifestations of depression. One area that has received comparatively less attention is the investigation of depression when it co-occurs with neurological disorders such as Parkinson's disease or Alzheimer's disease [25]. Aarsland et al. [2] emphasize that while Parkinson's disease (PD) is mainly recognized for its motor impairments, it also includes a wide range of non-motor symptoms, depression being among the most common, affecting about one-third of individuals with PD. Notably, depression in PD is often persistent and may even manifest during the prodromal phase [10].

The coexistence of depression with neurological disorders such as PD adds complexity to the diagnostic process and often results in underdiagnosis and inadequate treatment [21]. Despite growing interest in speech-based mental health assessment, the detection of depression from atypical speech remains an underexplored area. To date, only a few studies have specifically addressed this challenge. Ozkanca et al. [30] were among the first to investigate depression screening in PD patients using brief 10-second phoneme recordings. Their approach relied on handcrafted acoustic features combined with standard machine learning classifiers, demonstrating a promising relationship between vocal patterns and depression in PD. However, the study was limited in scope to isolated phoneme-level speech. In contrast, Pérez-Toro et al. [32–34] focused on longer speech samples, analyzing monologues from individuals with PD and Alzheimer's disease. They applied transfer learning strategies by first modeling affective states using ForestNet [35] in the valence-arousal space and then fine-tuning the models for depression detection. While their work demonstrates the potential of using emotion modeling as an intermediate task, it still leaves open questions regarding direct depression classification from atypical, disorder-specific speech. Together, these studies highlight a notable gap in the literature: the limited investigation into depression detection from neurologically atypical speech signals, where both motor and affective symptoms may alter vocal expression.

This study builds upon the work of Ruvolo et al. [36], who examined whether interpretable handcrafted acoustic features commonly used in automatic speech-based depression detection could be effectively applied to detect depression in

PD patients. Their analysis also compared acoustic descriptors from non-PD and PD speech to identify factors that might hinder accurate speech depression classification. For completeness, we present their findings and expand on their work by incorporating representations from state-of-the-art Speech Foundation Models (SFMs) to further explore the challenges of modeling depression in PD speech using such representations.

Using handcrafted features, we analyzed and compared the acoustic characteristics of individuals with comorbid Parkinson's disease and depression to those with depression alone, using two distinct corpora. In addition, we introduced a feature filtering method based on the Point Biserial Correlation Coefficient (PBCC) to identify the most informative features for depression detection, aiming to enhance classification performance. Finally, for clarity, we categorize the acoustic features into three main groups based on the type of information they represent: vocal source-related features, which influence pitch, loudness, and voice quality; vocal tract-related features, which reflect modifications in sound as it travels through the vocal tract, such as formants; and global-related features, which capture overall processes influencing speech production, like energy.

SFM-derived representations were used exclusively for detecting depression in individuals with Parkinson's disease. To assess the viability of these representations, we adopted the cross-validation-based layer selection approach proposed by Purohit et al. [31], originally developed for Parkinson's disease detection task.

The remainder of the paper is structured as follows: Sect. 2 describes the datasets used in the study. Section 3 outlines the methods explored, while Sect. 4 details the feature representations and experimental setup. Section 5 presents the experimental results, followed by a discussion and analysis in Sect. 6. Finally, Sect. 7 concludes the paper.

2 Dataset

(a) Depression in Parkinson's disease (PD-D) [32]: The dataset comprises speech recordings from 60 Colombian Spanish speakers, including 25 Depressive Parkinson's Disease (D-PD) patients and 35 Non-Depressive Parkinson's Disease (ND-PD) patients. Each participant was asked to deliver a monologue describing their daily routine. Following the recordings, a neurologist assessed their neurological condition using the Movement Disorders Society – Unified Parkinson's Disease Rating Scale (MDS–UPDRS) [16], which is the standard tool for evaluating the neurological state of PD patients. The initial section of the MDS-UPDRS includes an item that evaluates depression based on daily routine activities, assigning scores from 0 to 4. Participants scoring above zero were categorized as D-PD, while those with a score of zero were identified as ND-PD. The average length of the monologues is $84{\pm}34$ s for D-PD and $80{\pm}37$ s for ND-PD, resulting in a total dataset duration of approximately 4892 s. Speaker 52 was excluded from the analysis due to recording issues.

(b) Distress analysis interview corpus - Wizard of Oz (DAIC-WOZ) [17]: The dataset includes audio-visual interviews from 189 participants who were

evaluated for psychological distress, amounting to 17 h of audio data. Each participant was assigned a self-assessed depression score based on the Patient Health Questionnaire (PHQ-8) method [23]. For our experiments, we extracted only the participants' speech recordings using the time labels provided in the dataset. Sessions 318, 321, 341, and 362 were excluded from the training set due to time-labelling errors.

Table 1 summarizes the two datasets.

Table 1. Distribution of utterances used in the study, corresponding to each label.

Database	Content	Depressed patients	Not-Depressed patients	Total
DAIC-WOZ	English	42	100	142
PD-D	Spanish	24	35	59

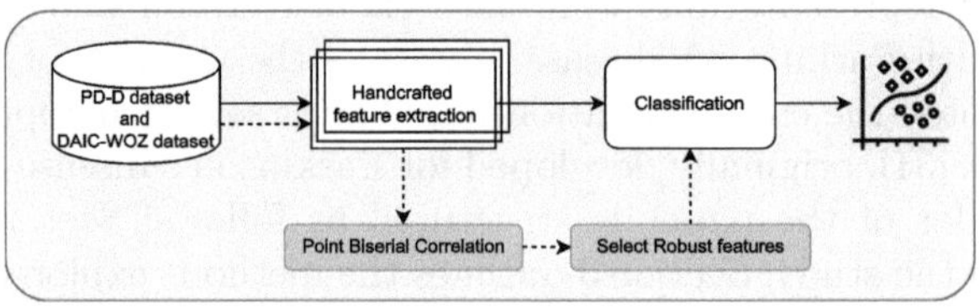

Fig. 1. Proposed methodologies representation: conventional approach (solid arrows) and PBCC-based approach (dashed arrows).

3 Methodology

This study employs two distinct approaches, which are outlined below.

3.1 Feature Selection for Handcrafted Acoustic Descriptors

As a baseline approach, handcrafted features were initially extracted from the input audio signal and used as input representations for the classifier module to produce confidence scores (see solid arrows in Fig. 1). This method provides a useful point of comparison with more sophisticated architectures.

Building upon the handcrafted features approach, we introduce a feature selection step to refine the input representation. After extracting features from the raw audio signal, we apply the Point Biserial Correlation Coefficient (PBCC) to identify the most informative subset of features (see dashed arrows in Fig. 1). PBCC measures the strength of the linear association between a binary target variable (D/ND) and continuous-valued features, enabling the selection of features that are most relevant for classification.

The PBCC is defined as:

$$r_{pb} = \frac{M_D - M_{ND}}{s_n}\sqrt{\frac{n_D n_{ND}}{n^2}}$$

where M_D and M_{ND} denote the mean feature values for the Depressive (D) and Non-Depressive (ND) classes, respectively; n_D and n_{ND} are the number of samples in each class; n is the total number of samples; and s_n is the standard deviation of the feature values across all samples.

To begin with, a range of correlation thresholds is defined. For each threshold value, the PBCC is calculated between every feature and the target labels in the training set. Features that exceed the given threshold are retained, as they demonstrate a stronger linear association with the class labels and are considered more discriminative.

Next, a Gradient Boosting (GB) classifier is employed to evaluate the predictive performance of the selected feature subsets. Thresholds ranging from 0.06 to 0.6, with increments of 0.2, are tested to determine which subset yields the highest classification accuracy.

3.2 Cross Validation Based Layer Selection for SFMs

The proposed architecture consists of two main components: an upstream SFM encoder and a downstream classification module. The upstream encoder comprises a stack of N transformer layers, each incorporating self-attention mechanisms. The downstream module includes an average pooling layer followed by a fully connected multilayer perceptron (MLP).

To determine which encoder layer produces the most task-relevant representations, we adopt a simple yet effective procedure: (i) Representations are extracted from each layer of the SFM encoder using the input speech utterances. (ii) The downstream network is trained using these representations to perform the required task, and its performance is evaluated exclusively on the cross-validation set. (iii) The accuracy on the cross-validation set serves as a proxy for the effectiveness of the representations in capturing task-specific information. (iv) The layer that achieves the highest cross-validation accuracy is selected for final evaluation on the test set.

We now detail the training procedure for the proposed model.

Let X represent the input speech signal and $c \in \{D, ND\}$ the corresponding class label. The objective is to estimate the posterior probability $P(c|X)$

$$\begin{aligned} H_L &= \mathrm{ENC}_L(X; \theta_{e_L}), \\ P(c|X) &= \mathrm{softmax}(\mathrm{MLP}(\mathrm{Pool}(H_L); \theta_m)) \ \forall c \end{aligned} \tag{1}$$

Here, $H_L \in \mathbb{R}^{T \times D}$ denotes the sequence of embeddings from the L-th layer of the encoder, where T is the sequence length and D the embedding dimension. $\mathrm{ENC}_L(\cdot)$ is the encoder function for layer $L \in \{1, \ldots, N\}$ with parameters θ_{e_L}.

The pooling function Pool(·) aggregates the sequence of embeddings into a fixed-length representation, which is then passed through the MLP, parameterized by θ_m, followed by a softmax to produce the class probabilities.

The predicted label $\hat{c}$ is assigned by selecting the class with the highest posterior probability:

$$\hat{c} = \arg\max_{c} P(c|X)$$

Model training is guided by minimizing the cross-entropy loss $\mathcal{L}$ between the predicted distribution $P(c|X)$ and the ground truth label c:

$$\mathcal{L} = -\log P(c|X)$$

The encoder parameters θ_{e_L} are initialized using weights from a pretrained model and remain frozen during training. In contrast, the downstream parameters θ_m are randomly initialized and optimized during training.

4 Feature Description and Training Protocol

In this section, we provide a brief overview of the handcrafted features and SFMs used in this study, along with the training protocol applied for each setup.

4.1 Handcrafted Features

This study utilizes three widely recognized sets of knowledge-driven handcrafted features: eGeMAPS [13], ComParE [37], and DisVoice [29]. The eGeMAPS set comprises 25 Low-Level Descriptors (LLDs) that capture essential acoustic properties, including frequency, energy, amplitude, and spectral characteristics. These descriptors are further processed using a set of statistical functionals, yielding a total of 88 features. ComParE provides a significantly larger feature set, comprising 6373 descriptors that include delta coefficients at the frame level and statistical functionals at the utterance level, all extracted via the openSMILE toolkit [12]. DisVoice features, on the other hand, combine static representations related to phonation, articulation, and prosody into a unified feature vector. Further details and extraction procedures are available in [29].

For the classification task, we employed three machine learning algorithms: Support Vector Machine (SVM), Random Forest (RF), and Gradient Boosting (GB). Hyperparameters for each model were optimized using grid search in conjunction with 6-fold cross-validation, ensuring reliable and robust model selection.

To maintain consistency with prior work [32], we employed the Leave-One-Speaker-Out (LOSO) cross-validation protocol for the PD-D corpus. Specifically, for evaluating the k-th speaker, the model was trained on data from the remaining $k-1$ speakers. For the DIAC dataset, evaluations were conducted on the development set, as the official test set was reserved for the AVEC 2016 challenge [40].

4.2 SFM Based Features

In this work, we investigate two Speech Foundation Models (SFMs) for the task of PD-D detection. These models were deliberately chosen to facilitate a comparative analysis of the impact of monolingual versus multilingual pertaining, a relevant factor given that the PD-D corpus comprises Spanish-language recordings.

Wav2vec2.0-base [3], hereafter referred to as W2V2, adopts a self-supervised learning framework that integrates contrastive learning with masked prediction. The model architecture consists of 12 transformer encoder layers with 768-dimensional hidden states and 8 attention heads, totaling approximately 95 million parameters. It was pretrained on 960 h of English speech from the LibriSpeech corpus.

XLSR [5] is a multilingual extension of Wav2vec2.0, featuring 24 transformer encoder layers, 1024-dimensional hidden states, and 16 attention heads, resulting in a model size of 315 million parameters. It was pretrained on speech data spanning 53 languages.

The Speech Foundation Models (SFMs) were obtained from HuggingFace. The downstream head composed of a single hidden layer with 256 nodes and an output layer of 2 nodes, corresponding to the two target classes (Healthy Control [HC] and Parkinson's Disease [PD]). The hidden layer employed ReLU activation, while the output layer used a softmax activation to produce class probabilities. Model training was performed using the Adam optimizer and cross-entropy loss. A batch size of 4 was used, with gradient accumulation set to 8 and the seed value was set to 1337. During probing for the downstream classification task, a learning rate of 5×10^{-4} was used for W2V2, and 1×10^{-4} for XLSR.

To evaluate the PD-D corpus using the SFM layer selection approach, we employed a 5-fold cross-validation strategy. Each fold consisted of speaker-independent training, validation, and test sets, comprising 35, 12, and 12 samples respectively.

5 System Performance

This section reports the results and examines the classification performance associated with each feature category.

5.1 Hancrafted Features

Table 2 summarizes the results obtained using the best-performing classifier (Gradient Boosting, GB) for each feature set across both corpora considered in this study. In the DAIC-WOZ dataset, our proposed system substantially outperforms the baseline results reported in the AVEC 2016 challenge, which were based on the eGeMAPS feature set with an SVM classifier, achieving an improvement of approximately 51% in F1-score. While the conventional use of eGeMAPS yields an F1-score of 0.74, performance slightly drops to 0.69 following feature selection, likely due to the limited dimensionality of the feature set. Conversely, both ComPARE and *DisVoice* show marked performance gains after applying feature selection.

Table 2. Classifiers' performance over the two datasets. *Dims* denotes the feature dimension; *Thr.* signifies the threshold set for feature selection; *D* and *ND* denote depressed and not-depressed patients, respectively; *O* is the unweighted average of *D* and *ND*.

Features	Dims	Thr.	F1-score			Precision		Recall	
			O	D	ND	D	ND	D	ND
DAIC-Woz									
Valstar et al. [40]	88		0.49	0.41	0.58	0.26	0.94	0.88	0.42
Conventional approach									
eGeMAPS	88		**0.74**	0.62	0.87	0.90	0.78	0.47	0.97
ComPARE	6373		0.47	0.24	0.70	0.45	0.59	0.16	0.86
DisVoice	620		0.55	0.33	0.77	0.50	0.69	0.25	0.87
Feature-selection approach									
eGeMAPS	39	0.18	0.69	0.54	0.84	0.67	0.72	0.33	0.91
ComPARE	2756	0.18	**0.72**	0.65	0.80	0.62	0.78	0.33	0.87
DisVoice	184	0.20	0.65	0.47	0.83	0.80	0.73	0.33	0.96
PD-D									
Perez-Toro et al. [32]			0.68	-	-	-	-	-	-
Conventional approach									
eGeMAPS	88		0.54	0.40	0.69	0.53	0.61	0.32	0.79
ComPARE	6373		0.43	0.30	0.56	0.33	0.53	0.28	0.59
DisVoice	620		**0.74**	0.69	0.78	0.71	0.77	0.68	0.79
Feature-selection approach									
eGeMAPS	7	0.26	0.65	0.57	0.72	0.62	0.68	0.52	0.76
ComPARE	186	0.3	**0.78**	0.75	0.81	0.73	0.82	0.76	0.79
DisVoice	16	0.32	0.77	0.73	0.81	0.75	0.80	0.72	0.82

For the PD-D corpus, our methods surpass the overall F1-score of 0.70 reported by Pérez-Toro et al. [32], who employed Valence and Arousal representations for classification. Among the conventional approaches, *DisVoice* features initially exhibit the highest performance with an F1-score of 0.74. However, applying Point-Biserial Correlation Coefficient (PBCC)-based feature selection leads to significant improvements across all feature sets. In particular, ComPARE improves from 0.43 to 0.78 while using a reduced subset of just 186 features.

Overall, these findings demonstrate that PBCC-based feature selection effectively enhances classifier performance, especially in identifying depressed (D) patients. The only exception is the slight decline observed for eGeMAPS in the

DAIC-WOZ dataset. These results highlight the benefit of filtering out redundant or non-informative features, enabling the development of more compact, interpretable, and discriminative models.

5.2 SFM Based Features

Figure 2 illustrates the accuracy trends of the two SFMs based on layer-wise analysis conducted over 5-fold cross-validation. The results indicate that Layer 6 yields the highest performance for W2V2, while Layer 16 is optimal for XLSR.

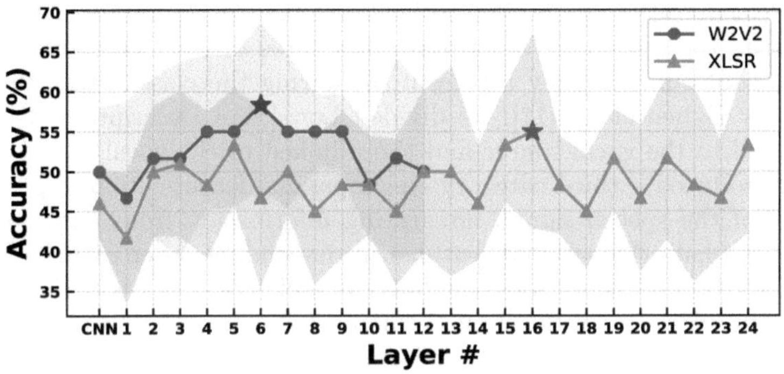

Fig. 2. -●-*on curves depicts mean of classification accuracy over 5 folds on validation-set at every layer. Best Accuracy (on validation-set data):* -★- *W2V2: 58.33%, and* -★- *XLSR: 55.00% from layer 6, and 16 respectively.*

Table 3 presents the test-set results on the PD-D corpus using the layers selected through the cross-validation-based layer selection strategy. The findings clearly indicate that the SFM-derived representations alone do not yield satisfactory performance for this task. Notably, the XLSR model pretrained on multiple languages including Spanish achieves an unweighted average F1-score of 40%, whereas the W2V2 model, pretrained solely on English, attains a higher score of 45%.

Table 3. SFM performance for the selected layer on test-set, *Dims* denotes the feature dimension; *D* and *ND* denote depressed and not-depressed patients, respectively; *O* is the unweighted average of *D* and *ND*.

Features	Dim.	F1-score			Precision		Recall	
		O	D	ND	D	ND	D	ND
PD-D								
W2v2 (L 6)	768	0.45	0.19	0.70	0.43	0.58	0.12	0.88
XLSR (L 16)	1024	0.40	0.12	0.67	0.29	0.56	0.08	0.85

6 Result Analysis and Discussion

This section offers a detailed analysis and interpretation of the results reported in the previous section.

6.1 Hancrafted Features

Building on the classification results from handcrafted features, we carried out a feature importance analysis by identifying the top 10 features according to their normalized importance scores, as determined by the best-performing classifier from the feature selection pipeline on both datasets. To facilitate interpretation, we organized these acoustic descriptors into three distinct categories based on the type of information they represent. Following the classification framework proposed by Eyben et al. [11], we divided Low-Level Descriptors (LLDs) into those related to the vocal source and those linked to the vocal tract. Additionally, we introduced a third category encompassing features that capture global properties of the speech signal, integrating information from both source and tract. Table 4 lists the selected features in descending order of importance, as assigned by the Gradient Boosting (GB) model. For reference, the descriptor names are provided, with the 'Index' column indicating the position of the feature in the `openSMILE` feature list, and the 'Group' column showing the assigned category.

The feature rankings in Table 4 reveal a distinct pattern in how the classifier identifies depression in speech from individuals with and without Parkinson's disease. In the DAIC-WOZ corpus, which involves classifying depressive versus healthy control subjects, the classifier places the greatest emphasis on source-related features—accounting for 6 out of the top 10. This is followed by a smaller number of vocal tract features (3 out of 10) and just one global low-level descriptor (LLD). The prominence of source-related features suggests that vocal characteristics tied to the stability and quality of vocal fold vibrations such as: jitter, harmonic-to-noise ratio, and pitch variability are particularly informative for depression detection in a neurologically healthy population. These results align with clinical findings, such as those by Hollien [20], who reported pitch alterations in depressed individuals, and Darby [8], who noted diminished pitch range and vocal intensity among depressed patients.

In contrast, the feature rankings for the PD-D dataset indicate a broader spread of informative features. Notably, the presence of several spectral features such as: spectral entropy, spectral centroid, spectral roll-off, spectral flux, and spectral kurtosis—reflects the vocal instability often observed in individuals with Parkinson's disease [18]. The observed reductions in spectral entropy and spectral centroid among depressed patients further highlight the nuanced interplay between emotional states and vocal quality [22]. Additionally, the feature Length L1, which captures aspects of voice quality and consistency, is significantly impacted, pointing to irregular speech patterns likely caused by motor impairments. Overall, this distribution underscores the added complexity in

Table 4. Feature ranking of GB trained on ComParE for both DAIC-WOZ (left) and PD-D (right), using PBCC feature selection approach.

DAIC-WOZ			PD-D		
Index	LLD name	Group	Index	LLD name	Group
3861	logHNR	Source	142	Length L1	Global
4038	Jitter DDP	Source	88	RMS Energy	Global
5126	Py Sharpness	Source	1	Length L1	Global
1493	Spectral Harmonicity	Source	64	RMS Energy	Global
6077	Spectral Variance	Global	6067	Spectral Entropy	Vocal tract
6174	MFCC	Vocal tract	1245	Spectral Flux	Global
2365	audSpec	Vocal tract	1476	Py Sharpness	Source
4132	F0	Source	2925	Spectral RollOff 90.0	Vocal tract
4131	F0	Source	2991	Spectral Centroid	Global
1373	Spectral Skeweness	Vocal tract	3106	Spectral Kurtosis	Global

detecting depression in PD patients due to the interplay between emotional and motor-related vocal alterations.

6.2 SFM Based Features

While handcrafted acoustic features enable interpretability and facilitate detailed analysis, such transparency is not readily achievable with representations derived from SFMs. Interestingly, contrary to earlier findings where SFM-based features have outperformed handcrafted ones for tasks like depression detection [42] and Parkinson's disease classification [14,31], this performance advantage diminishes in scenarios where depression coexists with Parkinson's disease. One possible explanation lies in the limitations of SFMs, which are typically pretrained on large-scale general speech corpora and may thus lack sensitivity to the subtle interplay between affective cues and motor deficits characteristic of this comorbid condition. The performances obtained further support this observation, for instance, when we analyse the mean sensitivity (correct classification rate for PD-D) and specificity (correct classification rate for PD-ND) scores across five folds, we observe a high specificity of 82% and a notably low sensitivity of 24% for W2V2 (L 6). This imbalance hints at the model's bias toward the majority class and its difficulty in capturing information related to depression within the pathological speech condition. Overfitting to the training data may also contribute to this limitation. To address these issues, future work will explore data augmentation and balancing strategies aimed at improving model robustness and sensitivity to underrepresented classes.

7 Conclusion

This study investigates automatic depression detection in individuals with Parkinson's disease (PD) using the PD Depression (PD-D) corpus. We explore two distinct feature types for this work: (1) interpretable, knowledge-based handcrafted acoustic representations, and (2) non-interpretable features derived from Speech Foundation Models (SFMs). For the handcrafted feature analysis, we not only evaluate their performance on the PD-D corpus but also study and compare acoustic descriptor patterns with those observed in typical depression-affected speech using the DAIC-WOZ corpus. The evaluation of SFM-derived features is focused exclusively on the PD-D dataset to assess their effectiveness in detecting depression within atypical speech associated with PD.

The classification results indicate that handcrafted feature-based approaches, such as those using the ComParE feature set, can achieve an F1-score of 43% for depression detection in individuals with Parkinson's disease. Notably, performance improves substantially with the F1-score rising to 78% when redundant features are removed using a Point Biserial Correlation-based feature selection strategy. These findings highlight the critical role of feature selection in enhancing model robustness and discriminative power. In contrast, the performance of SFM-derived features remains subpar, even when representations are extracted from the optimal encoder layer identified via cross-validation layer selection methodology. The results indicate that these models tend to exhibit a bias toward the majority class, indicating limited effectiveness in capturing depression-related cues within the atypical speech patterns of individuals with Parkinson's disease.

The analysis of feature rankings (using handcrafted features) highlights distinct acoustic profiles of depression in non-PD versus PD speech. In the DAIC-WOZ dataset, the classifier places strong emphasis on source-related features, underscoring their critical role in detecting depressive states an insight consistent with prior studies showing that vocal fluctuations, such as pitch variability, are reliable markers of depression. Whereas, speech from individuals with Parkinson's disease exhibits a wider prominence of spectral features, reflecting the intricate speech alterations associated with the motor symptoms characteristic of the disorder.

Our findings suggest that the presence of Parkinson's disease complicates the automatic classification of depression, likely due to overlapping and interacting acoustic symptoms. The study demonstrates that depression manifests differently in the speech of individuals with Parkinson's compared to those without, emphasizing the need for tailored approaches in speech-based mental health assessment. Our results demonstrate that handcrafted features tend to yield better PD-D detection than SFM-derived representations. To better leverage the potential of SFMs, future work will focus on exploring data augmentation strategies aimed at addressing both the limited data availability and class imbalance inherent in the PD-D dataset.

One limitation of this study is the reliance on a low-resource and imbalanced dataset, where depression labeling is based solely on a non-zero score for the

"Depressed mood" item in the MDS–UPDRS scale. We believe, a more robust labeling criterion would be necessary to enhance the reliability of the ground truth. Additionally, the dataset does not include information on medication status or speech-related subscores, both of which could provide valuable context for experimental design and interpretation of results. Addressing these limitations would require a separate dedicated data collection in the future.

Acknowledgment. This work was partially funded by (a) the SNSF through the Bridge Discovery project EMIL: Emotion in the loop - a step towards a comprehensive closed-loop deep brain stimulation in Parkinsonn's disease (grant no. $40B2\text{–}0\_194794$), and (b) CODI at UdeA, grant # PI2023-58010.

References

1. Global health estimates: Life expectancy and leading causes of death and disability. https://www.who.int/health-topics/mental-health. Accessed 15 Jan 2025
2. Aarsland, D., Påhlhagen, S., Ballard, C., Ehrt, U., Svenningsson, P.: Depression in Parkinson disease—epidemiology, mechanisms and management. Nat. Rev. Neurol. (2012)
3. Baevski, A., Zhou, Y., Mohamed, A., Auli, M.: wav2vec 2.0: A framework for self-supervised learning of speech representations. In: Advances in Neural Information Processing Systems (2020)
4. Burdick, B., Holmes, C., Waln, R.: Recognition of suicide signs by physicians in different areas of specialization. J. Med. Educ. (1983)
5. Conneau, A., Baevski, A., Collobert, R., Mohamed, A., Auli, M.: Unsupervised cross-lingual representation learning for speech recognition. In: Interspeech (2021)
6. Cummins, N., Scherer, S., Krajewski, J., Schnieder, S., Epps, J., Quatieri, T.: A review of depression and suicide risk assessment using speech analysis. Speech Communication (2015)
7. Cummins, N., et al.: An investigation of depressed speech detection: features and normalization. In: Proceedings of INTERSPEECH (2011)
8. Darby, J., Simmons, N., Berger, P.: Speech and voice parameters of depression: a pilot study. J. Commun. Disord. (1984)
9. Dubagunta, S., Vlasenko, B., Doss, M.: Learning voice source related information for depression detection. In: Proceedings of ICASSP (2019)
10. Dušek, P., et al.: Relations of non-motor symptoms and dopamine transporter binding in rem sleep behavior disorder. Nat. Sci. Rep. (2019)
11. Eyben, F., Eyben, F.: Acoustic features and modelling (2016)
12. Eyben, F., Wöllmer, M., Schuller, B.: Opensmile: the Munich versatile and fast open-source audio feature extractor. In: Proceedings Of The 18th ACM International Conference On Multimedia (2010)
13. Eyben, F., et al.: The Geneva minimalistic acoustic parameter set (gemaps) for voice research and affective computing. IEEE Trans. Affect. Comput. (2015)
14. Favaro, A., et al.: Interpretable speech features vs. DNN embeddings: what to use in the automatic assessment of Parkinson's disease in multi-lingual scenarios. Comput. Biol. Med. (2023)
15. France, D., et al.: Acoustical properties of speech as indicators of depression and suicidal risk. IEEE Trans. Biomed. Eng. (2000)

16. Goetz, C., et al.: Movement disorder society-sponsored revision of the unified Parkinson's disease rating scale (MDS-UPDRS): scale presentation and clinimetric testing results. Off. J. Move. Disord. Soc. (2008)
17. Gratch, J., et al.: The distress analysis interview corpus of human and computer interviews. In: LREC (2014)
18. Hauptman, Y., et al.: Identifying distinctive acoustic and spectral features in Parkinson's disease. In: Proceedings of INTERSPEECH (2019)
19. He, L., Cao, C.: Automated depression analysis using convolutional neural networks from speech. J. Biomed. Inform. (2018)
20. Hollien, H.: Vocal indicators of psychological stress. Anna. N. Y. Acad. Sci. (1980)
21. Hussain, M., et al.: Similarities between depression and neurodegenerative diseases: pathophysiology, challenges in diagnosis and treatment options. Cureus (2020)
22. Hussenbocus, A., et al.: Statistical differences in speech acoustics of major depressed and non-depressed adolescents. In: Proceedings of ICSPCS (2015)
23. Kroenke, K., Strine, T.W., Spitzer, R.L., Williams, J.B., Berry, J.T., Mokdad, A.H.: The PHQ-8 as a measure of current depression in the general population. J. Affect. Disord. (2009)
24. Landau, M.: Acoustical properties of speech as indicators of depression and suicidal risk. Vanderbilt Undergraduate Res. J. (2008)
25. Lee, H., Lyketsos, C.: Depression in Alzheimer's disease: heterogeneity and related issues. Biol. Psychiatr. (2003)
26. Ma, X., et al.: Depaudionet: an efficient deep model for audio based depression classification. In: Proceedings of AVEC, On ACM MM (2016)
27. Moore II, E., et al.: Critical analysis of the impact of glottal features in the classification of clinical depression in speech. IEEE Trans. Biomed. Eng. (2007)
28. Nilsonne, A., et al.: Measuring the rate of change of voice fundamental frequency in fluent speech during mental depression. J. Acoust. Soc. Am. (1988)
29. Orozco-Arroyave, J.R., et al.: Neurospeech: an open-source software for Parkinson's speech analysis. Digit. Sig. Process. (2018)
30. Ozkanca, Y., Göksu öztürk, M., Ekmekci, M., Atkins, D., Demiroglu, C., Hosseini Ghomi, R.: Depression screening from voice samples of patients affected by Parkinson's disease. Digit. Biomarkers (2019)
31. Purohit, T., Ruvolo, B., Orozco-Arroyave, J.R., Magimai.-Doss, M.: Automatic Parkinson's disease detection from speech: layer selection vs adaptation of foundation models. In: ICASSP 2025 - 2025 IEEE International Conference on Acoustics, Speech and Signal Processing (ICASSP) (2025)
32. Pérez-Toro, P., Vásquez-Correa, J., Bocklet, T., Nöth, E., Orozco-Arroyave, J.: User state modeling based on the arousal-valence plane: applications in customer satisfaction and health-care. IEEE Trans. Affect. Comput. (2021)
33. Pérez-Toro, P., et al.: Depression assessment in people with Parkinson's disease: the combination of acoustic features and natural language processing. Speech Communication (2022)
34. Pérez-Toro, P., et al.: Transferring quantified emotion knowledge for the detection of depression in Alzheimer's disease using forestnets. In: Proceedings of ICASSP (2023)
35. Rodríguez-Salas, D., et al.: Mapping ensembles of trees to sparse, interpretable multilayer perceptron networks. SN Comput. Sci. (2020)
36. Ruvolo, B., Purohit, T., Vlasenko, B., Orozco-Arroyave, J., Doss, M.: Exploring the complexity of Parkinson's patient speech for depression detection task: a qualitative analysis. In: Proceedings of Workshop on Speech Pathology Analysis and DEtection (SPADE 2025) (2025)

37. Schuller, B., et al.: The INTERSPEECH 2013 computational paralinguistics challenge: social signals, conflict, emotion, autism. In: Proceedings INTERSPEECH 2013, 14th Annual Conference of the International Speech Communication Association, Lyon, France (2013)
38. Scibelli, F., et al.: Depression speaks: automatic discrimination between depressed and non-depressed speakers based on nonverbal speech features. In: Proceedings of ICASSP (2018)
39. Stasak, B., et al.: An investigation of emotional speech in depression classification. In: Proceedings of INTERSPEECH (2016)
40. Valstar, M., et al.: AVEC 2016: depression, mood, and emotion recognition workshop and challenge. In: AVEC (2016)
41. World Health Organization: Depression. https://www.who.int/news-room/fact-sheets/detail/depression. Accessed 19 Oct 2023
42. Wu, W., Zhang, C., Woodland, P.C.: Self-supervised representations in speech-based depression detection. In: ICASSP 2023-2023 IEEE International Conference on Acoustics, Speech and Signal Processing (ICASSP). IEEE (2023)
43. Zahid, L., et al.: Detection of speech impairments in Parkinson disease using hand-crafted feature-based model on Spanish speech corpus. In: Proceedings of CCIS (2020)

Author Index

J. I. Godino Llorente (Ed.): AAPS 2024, CCIS 2646, p. 119, 2026.
https://doi.org/10.1007/978-3-032-07083-8

Author Index

[illegible] (Ed.): AAPS 2024, CCIS 2[illegible], p. 115, 2026.
https://doi.org/10.1007/978-3-032-07082-1

MIX
Papier aus verantwortungsvollen Quellen
Paper from responsible sources
FSC® C105338

If you have any concerns about our products,
you can contact us on
ProductSafety@springernature.com

In case Publisher is established outside the EU,
the EU authorized representative is:
Springer Nature Customer Service Center GmbH
Europaplatz 3, 69115 Heidelberg, Germany

Printed by Libri Plureos GmbH
in Hamburg, Germany